BEQOMING

BEQOMING

*Everything you didn't know
you wanted.*

AZRYA + BENJAMIN
BEQUER

BEQOMING
PUBLISHING

BEQOMING
Everything You Didn't Know You Wanted

ISBN 978-1-5445-2546-4 *Hardcover*
         978-1-5445-2545-7 *Paperback*
         978-1-5445-2544-0 *Ebook*
         978-1-5445-2644-7 *Audiobook*

May this book plug you into the pulse of the profound.

Az: *To my grandmother, Mutzi, who forged me through her love, and to all the trees and grasses who welcomed me home.*

Bee: *To my father, Bello, whose faith in me gave me the courage to step into shoes that I did not know I could fill. His loyalty was the anchor that grounded me. His unwavering love gave me the inspiration to manifest my dreams into reality. His example showed me the way. I am grateful to have his blood coursing through my veins.*

We: *To the Indigenous peoples who kept the umbilical cord to our ancient Mother intact. Thank you for preserving and sharing your sacred ways.*

We are remembering.

CONTENTS

PART 1. STRIPPED AWAKE

PART 2. RELENTLESS DEVOTION

PART 3. DIE BEFORE YOU DIE

B≡QOMING

(NOUN | VERB) *be·com·ing*

devotion to the process of becoming who you are designed to be by radically embracing your greatest challenges as curriculum and savoring the full spectrum of life

DEVOURED

"We are alive only to the degree to which
we are willing to be annihilated."

—Glennon Doyle, *Untamed*

Bee (a.k.a. Benjamin): *Azrya and I sit beachfront at a boutique resort in Tulum, Mexico, watching the midday sun glitter on the turquoise sea as the LSD starts to kick in.*

We've chosen to journey into an altered state of consciousness together because we know LSD—despite its many negative connotations and marred reputation—has the capacity to facilitate profound intimacy when ingested intentionally.

The depth of our brand-new connection is thick, even in the silence. It oozes with potential and risk. Truth is, I'm still unsure of what to make of this little punk rock hippie alien priestess that walked into my life two weeks ago and captivated me with her fearless self-expression, radical world views, and ancient eyes. She's not my usual type, with her European white skin and an awareness that comes from the deepest recesses of her consciousness. Despite how profoundly magnetized I am to her, red flags urge me to protect my heart. This woman is a wild card; she doesn't play by the rules.

Her fierce independence and rejection of all things conventional indicate a potential misalignment between what I want and what she's authentically ready to give in terms of long-term commitment. Her invitation for me to lean into the uncertainty of her heart is one I am wary of. This could get messy, and I am still scarred from having rushed into romance before.

And yet...despite how much she terrifies me, all I want to do is devour her.

I excuse myself, telling her I'm heading to the restroom. Instead, I go back to our casita to prepare a little surprise for her, the woman who would change the trajectory of my life forever.

Azrya: *Not long after Benjamin leaves, the sky begins to change in color. The first few drops of warm rain send beachgoers into a mad dash of gathering their belongings and finding shelter.*

But not me.

I cover our valuables with a towel, strip off my bikini top, and walk toward the churning waves, welcoming the tropical storm with every inch of my tingling skin. The LSD is expanding my bandwidth of sensory perception, and the sudden change in climate feels like a cosmic invitation, beckoning me to remember my untamed, erotic innocence.

I come to a stop at the water's edge, raising my hands toward the sky.

I am consumed by my intense attraction to Benjamin, infused with a quiet awareness that allowing myself to fully lean into the force field of his masculine presence might come at a cost.

I've been playing it safe, keeping an energetic distance, feeling like I need to evaluate further whether the glaring gap between who we are at our core is too big to close. But now, the psychoactive medicine is dissolving my ego's attempts to grasp at control.

All I want is for him to devour me.

Then: he appears beside me, his energy catapulting me back into the present moment. We are now the last ones standing on the deserted beach. His eyes are on fire. Wordlessly, he gestures toward the water. He doesn't have to tell me twice.

We embrace, swirling in the exquisite, bathtub-warm waves. I cling to his broad shoulders like I've just found land after a lifetime of floating in the sea. Rain drips down our faces. The expansiveness of the cosmos pulsates between our warm bodies. It's perfection.

As we emerge from the ocean, laughing and quaking with aliveness and turn-on, I feel sensations beyond what I can describe. Benjamin and I make our way back to our casita, raindrops and ocean salt pearling on our sun-kissed skin.

He opens the door, and I step inside to find candles illuminating the darkened space. Before I have a chance to get my bearings, Benjamin approaches me with a sudden intensity.

He's holding something in his hand. It takes me a moment to realize what it is.

Bee: *"If you take this blindfold," I say to Azrya, who is staring at me, dripping and wide-eyed, "you are agreeing to surrender to me. What that means is this: I will tie you up, push your boundaries of pleasure and pain, and have my way with you. But there's one very important rule, so listen closely. You may communicate only in sounds, not words. You can say 'stop' at any point. Just know that if you do, the experience is over, and will not begin again under any circumstances, end of story. Do you choose to fully surrender to me?"*

The electricity between us is so palpable I can taste it. Azrya looks down at the blindfold in my hand, and I can feel her heart rate speed up. This is an edge for her, which is exactly how I like it. Her usual poise and effortless confidence are rattled, and she's into it. Few people can push her out of her comfort zone, and I just did. Hard.

She looks me straight in the eyes, the LSD now peaking in our system. I can see she accepts the challenge. She intuitively understands the empowerment that is available to her in the choice to willingly surrender to the unknown.

She grasps the magnitude of the true act of courage that it requires to relinquish this kind of control.

She takes the blindfold, consenting to my invitation without saying a word.

"Get undressed," I command.

Azrya: *His warm, thick hands secure my delicate ankles and wrists into the straps attached to the four corners of the bed. This is a professional setup. I am so impressed that I briefly allow my mind to drift to the logistics required to make this happen.*

But the moment he places the blindfold on me and everything goes dark, it hits me just how vulnerable and exposed I am in this position, and I squeal with the intensity of anticipation teetering on the edge of panic—blindly tugging at my restraints, testing their resolve. I want to use words to diffuse the nervous energy pulsating through me, but I submit to the rules, so I allow my naked body to buck and quiver instead.

Iridescent colors of purple and blue glow inside of my blindfold. The caress of what feels like a feather tickles my nipples, alternating with gentle kisses on the curves of my skin. He tortures me with his breath, the flick of his tongue barely touching the most tender parts of me. My body explodes with the sensation of hot wax dripping on my belly and breasts, making me shriek, then collapse into anxious giggles. Bee's breath, his energy, his warmth envelop me.

In the cloud of his love, I feel the safety within the danger, and it leaves me gasping, awestruck.

Time disappears as the dance between pain and pleasure begins to annihilate me. Taken by hands infinitely stronger than my own, I discover a depth of surrender, of freedom, beyond my imagination.

I blossom.
I dissolve.
I BΞQOMΞ.

Once the experience is over, I feel like a kid getting off of a rollercoaster for the first time. My skin still stinging with sensual whip stains, he holds me like I've never been held. All I see is him. We lay in each other's arms, basking in the bliss of our chemistry, blasted open by love.

Then, the giggles and cuddles suddenly turn serious.

"I realized something profound today," Benjamin says. I sit up to look at him, hanging onto his every word. He continues, "My greatest fear was to die without having given myself completely to someone. And I realized today, that no matter what happens between us, I now know what that feels like. If I died tomorrow, I could die happy knowing that I loved so completely—even if just for a moment. That's the gift you've given me, and I'm forever grateful."

Emotion floods my body. I bow at the altar that is this man, as his heart cracks open.

"I can't imagine it ever getting any better," he says. "I can't imagine ever wanting anyone else. I give you my heart. Do with it what you will."

I gaze beyond his glowing eyes into the depths of his soul. "I will cherish it for the sacred gift that it is," I reply, my own heart gushing with love.

And suddenly, it's there.

The All In moment.

A puzzle piece clicks into place as I look into his eyes and finally recognize my King.

In his reflection, I find my Queen.

⬡ ⬡ ◇

We: And then we rode off into the sunset together, right? Isn't that how the ultimate fairy tale version of the story goes?

Not so quick.

Yes, that All In moment in Tulum was real. The LSD—like psyche-delics so reliably do—stripped away all the anxiety and inhibition that kept our hearts guarded and our egos in controlled evalua-tion. It allowed us to quantum leap our relationship while we were essentially still strangers by choosing to commit to each other in a potent, unfiltered moment of our Truest Truth. *And*—it was still an altered state of consciousness, therefore not a permanent state. Rather, it was a temporary opportunity to taste a lived experience of what is possible when we rise above fear and operate from a place of raw, undiluted love.

That moment fused us together. It acted as a portal for us to calibrate to a timeline of a shared future and catalyzed the most profound initiation of B≡QOMING in both of our lives. That moment catapulted us into the journey of collapsing the veil of what we *thought* we wanted, and discovering the uncharted (and often profoundly challenging) terrain of *everything we didn't know we wanted.* In this process we had been forced to confront all the parts of our own fear that threaten to pull us apart, to separate us from this state of Love. These fears are not unique to us, nor are we completely free of them, even as we write these words. They are universal fears. Fears that define humanity. The fear of losing that which is most precious; of heartbreak; of not being enough, of being too much; of devastating circumstances beyond our control. The fear of losing our identity, of being unable to provide and receive emotional and physical safety, of missing out on our truest potential and realizing too late we took a wrong turn. The fear of opening our hearts, of being truly seen, both in our magic and in our shit.

The ultimate fear: of letting Love *in.*

This book aims to reveal how all these universal human fears can become our greatest teachers, firstly by awakening us to the reality of how much power we give external circumstances over our lives.

Think about it. The collective self-worth of humanity hangs by a delicate thread, attached to a whole plethora of things we've been convinced to want, all of which can disappear in a heartbeat: money, status, appearance, job security, relationship security, environmental security.

Attaching your self-worth to these things is the epitome of unsustainability, for none of them are guaranteed to last. It is only through the full embracing of this truth that you can liberate yourself from your fears and attachments, and taste the true freedom that comes from sincerely *KNOWING who you are.*

This book speaks to the part of you that exists beyond your name, title, and identity. The part of you that is ready to be freed from any and all shackles of fear.

We, your authors—Benjamin and Azrya—have devoted our entire lives to this liberation process, and we've come to see our partnership as a microcosm of our larger relationship with life and the universe itself. Our story is both highly unique and deeply universal, in that it contains within it the same agonizing challenges and triumphs that everyone who chooses a path of true intimacy with self and others will inevitably be forced to confront.

For us, the journey of B Ξ Q O M I N G has been both gradual and abrupt. It has invigorated us and depleted us. It has taken us to the greatest heights and darkest lows. It has expanded our capacity to be with all of ourselves and each other, and more than anything, it has allowed us to remember how to not just learn to love ourselves and each other, but to *be Love.*

We're not sure there's anything more important than that.

This is why we've decided to share our personal story with you in great detail. Some of those details may make you wonder if you are reading a personal development book, a memoir, or an erotic fiction story. Our words might make you squirm a little—we believe that's a good thing. We're giving you an out-of-the-box, unflinchingly honest, real-time example of what it looks like to devote yourself to the path of B Ξ Q O M I N G—not just as individuals, but also in the crucible of intimate partnership and awakened union.

Sure, there have been times where we've questioned if we're going too far with our transparency, and whether it would be better to "tone it down a little" in an attempt to remain somewhat "appropriate" and make sure we don't offend anybody too much. Yet every time we've felt that hesitation energy, we reflected on our favorite Jim Dethmer question:

"What are you willing to risk for full aliveness?"

In the case of leaving this book raw and uncensored, we risk that you will not like us. We risk being seen as eccentric, reckless, self-obsessed, irrational, new-age, hedonistic exhibitionists. We risk that we make you, and the people we love, deeply uncomfortable.

But when we really move beyond our doubts, our answer to that question is always the same: *What we are willing to risk for full aliveness is **everything**.*

That's how committed we are to B Ξ Q O M I N G.

And we want the same for you.

We're inviting you to share the fullness of who you are with the world, by sharing the fullness of who we are with you. Life is the best author, and we are being asked to trust that the true stories of our B Ξ Q O M I N G are encoded with messages and lessons that will activate you in ways neither of us will ever understand.

Therefore, our promise is to hold nothing back and to never play it safe. To shatter the edge of our personal comfort zones. To not just embrace the taboo but celebrate it. To take you into the depths of our pain and our pleasure. To give you intimate access to our profound and our profane. To lay it all bare, from our farts to our fucks. To unapologetically claim *all* of ourselves as sacred, so that we may become unflinching mirrors of your own perfect imperfection.

For you, dear reader, we vow to be anything but "appropriate," for that is not where the Truest Truth resides.

And only the Truest Truth will set us free.

EVERYTHING YOU DIDN'T KNOW YOU WANTED

Do you find yourself having a lot of these conversations?

"Hey, how are you?"
"Fine thanks. You?"
"Pretty good, thanks."

Honestly. How many times a day do we robotically repeat this rehearsed, societally approved script back and forth to each other? Why aren't we answering with, "Fucking *spectacular*," or "I'm really struggling right now"?

What game are we *really* playing?

In our opinion, being "fine" is a tragedy.

You are the one sperm out of the 100 million that made it to the egg.

You are a molecular masterpiece that can shape and mold reality with the power of your thoughts and feelings.

You are a living, breathing, biological miracle. You didn't come here to be *fine*.

You didn't traverse the narrow passage of your mother's womb and gasp for air covered in blood and goo to be "pretty good."

You came to live fiercely and love unapologetically. To jump, fall, soar, and fall again. To milk every last drop of potential from this extraordinary thing called *your life*, and to leave a legacy that your great-grandchildren will speak of with awe and wonder when they proudly share about their lineage, feeling the warm echoes of your vibrant soul still surrounding them long after you're gone.

No matter what your path looks like, you came here to embody the magnificent radiance of your Truest Truth and follow it without hesitation. To give the gift you were designed to give, and to give it wholeheartedly.

As we begin this journey together, know that the path of B≡QOMING is full of paradoxes. The more you are willing to break open, the more whole you B Ξ Ọ O M Ξ. The more power-fully you learn to create whatever you want, the more you value the simplest of things. The more you face your own shadow, the more you begin to live in the light.

The more willing you are to let that which no longer serves you die, the more alive you B Ξ Ọ O M Ξ.

And the more you are able to dissolve the veil of what you *think* you want, the more you can begin to receive *everything you didn't know you wanted.*

So what do you *think* you want? All the obvious good stuff: hap-piness, security, ease, adventure, harmony, a sexy bod, confidence.

Or do you?

What if....

- You *think* you want happiness, and you do, but what you are *really* seeking is to savor your full-spectrum aliveness, which encompasses everything from the most heart-wrenching grief to the most awe-inspiring gratitude.

- You *think* you want to feel safe and secure, and you do, but a deeper part of your spirit is also craving the thrill of facing your shadow, taking real risks, and stepping outside of your comfort zone.

- You *think* you want things to be easy, and you do, but what you *really* want is to learn how to alchemize the unavoidable challenges of life into traction that can propel you into embodying who you were designed to be.

- You *think* you want novelty and adventures, and you do, but what you want even more is the ability to find the magic in the mundane, to discover the profound in the profane, and to make love to all the in-between moments of life's peak experiences.

- You *think* you want harmony in your relationships, and you do, but what you *really* want is an honest, authentic, and trustworthy reflection of yourself through the eyes of another, which will inherently trigger your deepest wounds and insecurities, forcing you to evolve.

- You *think* you want the six-pack, and you do, but what you *really* want is to feel at home in your body, to cultivate unshakeable trust in yourself to honor the most important vessel you've been given to steward, so that when you lie on your deathbed you can rest easy KNOWING that you cared for yourself with true devotion.

- You *think* you want the willpower to say no to the chocolate cake, and you do, but what you *really* want is the ability to be able to slow down enough to savor just one or two bites with so much presence that you genuinely don't desire any more, and the need for willpower goes obsolete.

- You *think* you want to have the education and training to be considered an exceptional leader, and you do, but what you *really* want is to trust the larger intelligence of life so much that you let it make decisions through you, and watch in awe as your vision, purpose, and creative power amplifies far beyond what you could have mustered up on your own.

See the pattern? It's not either, or. It's yes, *and*.

THE DAWNING OF A NEW REALITY

If you've ever stood on a beach and watched the waves roll in, you'll know that they are relentless. This collective B Ξ Q O M I N G process is like the ocean hitting the shore. Sometimes the waves come in with ferocity, violently crashing and spraying. Other times they are mild and slow, meandering in and out in no particular hurry. But even when the tide is low and the ocean becomes mirror-like, it will never remain stagnant. The waves will always keep on coming.

You can't argue with the ocean. But you can learn to surf in the waves. The same is true for life.

We cannot argue with or pretend away that our species is navigating a precarious tipping point moment in human history. It's a choice point of epic proportions, and one that demands us to B Ξ Q O M Ξ resilient to the ever-changing tides of our uncertain future.

The only thing that is guaranteed in all of this is that death will need to be confronted along the way. Both literally and metaphorically. We are here with you to make this difficult and necessary acknowledgement of the cycle of life and death and to transform the death in your life into something truly beautiful.

What awaits us on the other side of this breakdown to breakthrough?

We believe it will be the beginning of a new reality, one that is up to us as individuals to co-create. We do this through the power of our heartfelt imagination and the sincere dedication to breaking the chains of generational trauma that have enslaved humanity for far too long. We must do this so the next generation does not have to inherit the same wounds we took on from our parents and those who came before them.

Our collective BᗺQOMING will allow our children and our children's children to walk home safely at night, to receive vital nutrients from healthy soil, to bathe and drink in the purest of waters and gaze up at the clearest of skies, ready to channel their emotional intelligence into meaningful relationships, inspiring art, and purposeful inventions. We see generations living out their Truest purpose surrounded by unwavering love and support, growing in expansive, thriving environments.

Now, for you personally, this new reality could look something like you waking up in the morning, excited to intentionally pour yourself into a heart-centered mission greater than your bottom line. It could look like beginning your day by sitting down for a spacious, technology-free, nutrient-rich breakfast with your loved ones, your heart overflowing with gratitude and appreciation for what you *already* have.

Perhaps it looks like feeling nourished by the depth and intimacy you get to share with those closest to you. Savoring their intricate details, seeing them fully, and allowing yourself to be seen, free of masks and distractions.

Perhaps it looks like exploring uncharted territory, experiencing the thrill of pioneering the great mystery, being stretched and challenged in ways that activate your spirit and keep you on your toes as you discover a version of yourself that is deeply solid but never rigid.

We see your new reality embodied as you B Ξ Q O M Ξ one who is unwavering in your devotion to the essentials and who emanates a warmth that makes other people's nervous systems unwind in your presence, without you saying a single word.

This version of you can be someone for others to lean into and seek counsel from, can be a safe place not just because you are kind and trustworthy but because you've been willing to travel to the darkest places of your own mind, heart, and body and have come through on the other side, bathed in light. This is what qualifies you to be a safe haven for others, for we cannot guide someone to places we shy away from within ourselves.

Last but not least, in your new reality, you are surrounded by trust-worthy, inspiring allies who are walking the path alongside you, allowing you to rest your head on your pillow at night with the unwavering KNOWING that *you are not alone.*

So, while we can't possibly know who you are today, where you are starting your B Ξ Q O M I N G journey from, nor where it will lead you, we do know that new versions of you are ready to be born and that a new reality awaits you—one full of things you never knew you wanted. If any of the above has resonated with you, perhaps even touched something deep inside your soul that has been long-ing to be remembered, then you are in the right place.

Now, let's explore a few of the main threads we'll follow through this journey of B Ξ Q O M I N G.

DEVOTION & ALTERED STATES

They say all roads lead to Rome.

For us, the path of psychedelics and plant medicines, such as Ayahuasca and psilocybin, coupled with the path of devotion—both to our individual B Ξ Q O M I N G journeys as well as our committed partnership—has yielded the most potent, acceler-ated results. What we love most about these transformative paths is the very thing they have in common: *They both force us to surren-der our defenses and let ourselves be seen fully, in all of our magic and all of our mess.*

They give us nowhere to hide, and ultimately, no choice but to let the fuck go. Hallelujah!

The Path of Plant Medicine and Psychedelics

The term "plant medicine" is very broad, and can encompass everything from entheogens such as psilocybin and Ayahuasca to butter lettuce and oregano.

We will be using the term with reference to the psychoactive plant materials that the Indigenous people of the Americas—who have preserved a strong connection to the intelligence of Earth—have been using for medicinal purposes for generations.

So what is the difference between a drug and a plant medicine? We'd say you can only call it medicine if it's for the sake of healing and sincere expansion. We don't judge recreational use, for we have experienced firsthand the healing benefits of play, but we highly recommend that you don't underestimate the implications of altering your consciousness in unconscious environments, with unconscious people, or for insincere reasons. These are incredibly powerful tools, which can easily be abused. Generally, a synthetic drug such as MDMA or LSD—which can also be used as a medicine in the right "set and setting"—is useful precisely because its effects are more predictable and replicable. Organic plant materials will vary more in dosage and their effects, and are highly dependent on the energetics of the space and the person. It is rare for any two experiences to be the same.

The beauty of working with a plant-based medicine is that the spirit of the substance remains intact, which can be experienced almost like communicating with a very distinct personality.

Our exploration of these realms is mostly focused on the profound healing effects of psilocybin mushrooms and Ayahuasca, which is a thick, dark brew made from two different plant materials, a vine and a DMT-containing leaf.

Ayahuasca is a sophisticated healing modality that originates in the Amazon rainforest and has been an integral part of shamanic cultures for thousands of years, with various different traditions and lineages preserving it through time.

Besides its ability to tap our consciousness into the energetic realms and evoke multidimensional, visionary states, it is also a purgative medicine, which means it allows us to "purge" things such as trauma, fear, neurosis, and victimhood from our system. Sometimes this looks like vomiting, shaking, crying, sweating, twitching, or shitting.

Sounds like a party, right? Exactly.

From the very beginning of our union, Ayahuasca became almost like a third party in our dynamic. Azrya was working intensely with the medicine for several years, integrating it into her private coaching and retreat work. Benjamin had been feeling the call to revisit the medicine after an eight-year break and quickly discovered that this plant teacher—often referred to as "Mother," "Grandmother," or "The Medicine," was a huge puzzle piece to his BΞQOMING.

Together, we dove into the shamanic realms over and over again, receiving much of the information contained in this book through our journeys.

If it wasn't for our experiences with these altered states, this book would likely never have been written, nor would our lives be as they are today. We are forever grateful to the Indigenous peoples who have kept these ancient wisdom traditions alive in the face of great adversity, and it is our deepest commitment to protect and uphold the sacredness of these potent modalities with all of the work that we do.

We will delve more deeply into the subject of plant medicine in Chapter 9. There, we will provide a comprehensive overview of how to safely and effectively work with these altered states. **We are *not* recommending that anyone work with psychedelics or plant medicine.** Few are called sincerely to this path, and if you are one of them, we advise you to check with your doctor prior to embarking on any psychedelic journey to make sure it is safe for you to explore these modalities.

The Path of Committed Partnership

Individualism says, You have to love yourself first before you can love others. But The Second Mountain ethos says: You have to be loved first so you can understand love, and you have to see yourself actively loving others so that you know you are worthy of love.

—David Brooks, *The Second Mountain*

Many associate the path of spiritual growth with the lone seeker who opts out of the human experience and chooses instead to sit in an ashram or cave for years of abstinence in order to attain enlightenment. In some ways, this path might actually be easier than choosing to awaken while in a committed partnership. The intense energy of passion and polarity that is required to generate sexual chemistry and soul intimacy is by nature volatile and unpredictable and will inevitably involve emotional messiness that you can't just *namaste* your way out of.

We believe it's a core human calling to be in union, both with an intimate partner as well as with the intelligence of the universe itself—which is really the same thing. We personally can't imagine life without the thrilling push and pull of the opposing forces of polarity, which we will refer to as masculine and feminine in this book, and which you are welcome to call Alpha and Omega if you prefer terminology that is gender neutral.[1]

When you choose to step on the path of B ≡ Q O M I N G alongside your intimate partner, you are both opting *in* to the human experience, in all of its terror and all of its glory. Some of the deepest collective wounds exist between the masculine and the feminine energies, accumulated from generations of domination and suppression.

That said, if you have the emotional stamina to traverse their choppy waters, you will be rewarded and eventually find yourself basking in the most profound oasis of pure, unconditional love through the

---

1   From the teachings of Justin Patrick Pierce & Londin Angel Winters.

reflection of another human soul who sees you fully and chooses you wholeheartedly. The vehicle of intimate partnership then becomes your access point to the divine. It becomes your spiritual practice.

If you are wondering how the hell your current partner or spouse is ever going to be able to meet you on this path, don't worry. We will revisit that topic later in more detail. For now, trust us that your counterpart—whether it's someone who is already by your side or someone who is yet to step into your life—will be a mirror to your soul, someone who you can invite to meet and dance with you in the fullness and vastness of who you truly are.

Awakening in the crucible of committed partnership is a path of devotion, and it is not for the faint of heart.

If you are single and looking to call in a conscious partner, visit *www. BΞQOMING.me/tools* to access our *Soulmate* manifestation exercise.

Bee: Sometimes I think Azrya is more alien than human. But in my eyes, she is the most impressive and profound person I have ever met. Her heart is pure and permanently cracked wide open. As I observe her laser-like determination to expand her consciousness, I am reminded often of the story of Roger Bannister and the four-minute mile.

Before 1954, everyone believed that it wasn't possible for a human to run a four-minute mile. Then: Roger Bannister shattered that belief in three minutes, fifty-nine and four-tenths of a second. Athletes had seriously attempted to break the four-minute mile for at least half a century, and everyone accepted that there was a physical limit that kept humans from moving faster. In a split second, Bannister showed the world that the barrier was psychological, not physical.

Within a year, several runners had caught up to Bannister's record, and many more have achieved the feat in the decades since. Once Bannister gave the world a glimpse of what was possible, the collective shift in belief allowed many more runners to do what had previously been impossible in all of human history.

Azrya is my four-minute mile.

Being in partnership with her has shattered my limited perception of what it means to be powerful, simply through witnessing how she embodies love and compassion as her default state. She has shown me what's possible when we truly tap into the present moment, synchronize ourselves with the intelligence of the universe, and let it guide us with unwavering trust. She's the epitome of surrendered certainty and has mastered the art of *responding* versus *reacting*.

What that looks like on a daily basis is this: Let's say Azrya gets triggered or feels contraction around something. Instead of getting defensive and lashing out, she instead turns her attention within herself and takes time to process what she's experiencing.

Because she firmly believes she co-creates every situation, anything that triggers her becomes medicine for her, in that it illuminates a blind spot in her awareness. She knows that blind spots are related to a fear, an insecurity, or a pattern of behavior from the past that is ready to evolve, and so she relates to it as an opportunity rather than a nuisance. When she's clear about what's coming up from the trigger, she invites me into a conversation and calmly expresses what she's feeling. This doesn't mean she's always come to a place of agreeing with me, but it does mean that we can have endlessly interesting conversations around the root causes of our differing opinions rather than engage in arguments or fights.

Sometimes, those conversations force me to face off with my own deepest fears and insecurities. Azrya is a relentless mirror, which can be exhausting, but at the end of the day, she's always taking a stand for my greatness.

Azrya's empathy is through the roof and is especially impressive to witness when she's coaching someone. She can connect with people at a level that allows her to feel what they are feeling, step into their reality, tap into their frequency, and provide true guidance from a place of deep understanding. She can have a high-powered CEO in tears as she drills to the heart of an issue and helps him feel all the feels. And, as easily as she can tap into the individual, she can also tap into the collective, in a way that gives her great compassion for people, animals, and the planet.

In a famous scene from Jerry McGuire, Tom Cruise says to Renee Zellweger: "You complete me." While I don't believe that statement can be true—for it implies that we as individuals are not whole without another—being with Azrya has taught me that we can activate and enable each other to complete ourselves. ***Through our union, we can facilitate the embodiment of our highest expression.***

Through her reflection, I see the King I never dreamt I could be.

Azrya: Early on in our romance, a friend asked me: "If you had to pick one word to describe Benjamin's love—which one would it be?"

"Unwavering," I replied.

My answer would be the same today, although today I am more aware of what that actually means and how Benjamin's unwavering love has illuminated all the deepest parts of me that are terrified of fully receiving the depth of his potent heart.

I've also learned that often the thing that turns you on the most about someone is also the thing that scares the shit out of you.

From the very beginning, when I sat trembling at his kitchen table, 10 minutes into our first "date"—I felt intuitively that I had met my match. That this was someone who could keep up with the intensity of my hunger to B Ξ Ϙ O M Ξ, to claim a life path full of risk and romance, support me in turning all of my visions into reality, and facilitate the sexual awakening I had been calling in my entire life.

It was a lot to take in. Hence the trembling.

As I got to know Benjamin, I learned that while in many ways, he exudes a very traditional archetypal father energy, there's nothing cookie cutter about him. In my eyes, Benjamin is a sophisticated badass that breaks every mold and defies every box. He's the almost-200 pounds of muscle that unflinchingly texts *everyone* kissy face emoticons—including high-powered attorneys and no-nonsense executives. At formal functions, amidst a sea of suits and ties, he can somehow make his signature look of black jeans, black hoodie, a pair of Chucks, and a Yankees baseball hat work for the "business attire" specified on the invitation. His spreadsheets are works of art that make my hands clammy. His gaze can light up a room, and it can shoot daggers into your heart.

He's as shrewd as he is gentle. As wise as he is crass. His body is like a rock, his chest strong enough to endure the deepest emotional waters. His massive hands look permanently manicured, and whether he's using them to build an empire or make a woman squirt—it's always with great precision and intentionality.

He's the most hygienic person I've ever met, yet he doesn't mind getting down and dirty in the bedroom, and he embraces the sweat, the spit, and the cum with zero qualms.

Benjamin is infinitely complex, and in some ways very simple. He is full of paradoxes. And one thing is for sure:

He's got my attention.

In fact, he dominates my awareness. I don't experience a single second of my reality where he is not present. He is always with me, even when we're not physically together. We have merged. We are *one*.

This deep bonding is a merging of worlds for us. I am his initiation into the spiritual. He is my initiation into the physical. Together, we represent and embody a broad spectrum of the human experience.

It is Benjamin who powerfully invited me to join him in the crucible of devotion. The container of our lifetime commitment has become the ultimate medicine ceremony.

It is the altar at which we pray.

We: If you find yourself resonating with what we've shared so far, amazing. If you don't have a penchant for these extreme avenues of transformation, do not fret. By no means are any of these modalities requirements. If your Truest Truth is that you're meant to walk this road sober and solo, that's cool too. Again, there is no right or wrong method to BΞQOMING the fullness of *you*, and awakening through committed partnership and/or psychedelics and plant medicine are very specific paths that are by no means right for everyone. You can create profound shifts in your consciousness and life through the path of subtleties, whether that be meditation, movement, breath, or journaling practices.

However, even the more nuanced path will eventually push your edges in one way or another. Life did not design your BΞQOMING to be watered down, meek, and distilled; if that were the case, you would miss out on the rich soil of your subconscious and the initiations it has in store for you. Letting go at this level is no easy feat for the carefully constructed ego identities we've appointed to guard our hearts with such righteousness and vigilance.

We can miss out on golden opportunities for our B Ξ Q O MI N G when we let these identities and beliefs attempt to control our lives under the ego's guise of keeping us "safe and normal." Much of the B Ξ Q O MI N G journey is about disarming these built-in egoic defense mechanisms long enough to allow the Truest Truth of our unguarded heart to reclaim its rightful seat at the steering wheel of our precious lives.

These paths of psychedelic journeying and devotional partnership are exhilarating, can feel somewhat dangerous, and are incredibly gratifying for the warrior spirit within us—the one that thrives on challenge and feasts on change, embraces fear and commits to catalyzing itself awake. Yet despite the power of plant medicine and passionate love to awaken us, there is no quick-fix magic pill for B Ξ Q O MI N G. There are no "Three Guaranteed Steps to Waking Up in 30 Days," no textbook strategy. B Ξ Q O MI N G is a nonlinear birthing, a labor of love that will continue for as long as you are alive—and likely, well beyond that.

And, in our humble opinion, it's a goddamn privilege.

THE LANGUAGE OF B Ξ Q O MI N G

Before we dive in further, we're going to break down the meaning of B Ξ Q O MI N G and introduce you to a few other important words that we've defined in new ways to help you understand that which the English language hasn't properly been able to express (yet).

B ☰ Q O M I N G is a very different ball game than "becoming" as we know it. You can "become" sick of your job, "become" bored of your spouse, "become" annoyed with the news, or "become" proficient at Scrabble. These are all the regular, normalized ways of becoming.

B ☰ Q O M I N G, however, is a significant, soul-level process that takes up a lot of space—that's why we've written it in all capital letters.

First and foremost, the path of B ☰ Q O M I N G is defined by one thing: *questions*. We believe that a question well asked is a question half answered. Questions are powerful, and we will use them throughout this book to shape our understanding of the stories and wisdom we present.

On this journey, you must be willing to ask *why*. Over and over again. Only in questioning everything—even the things that seem obvious—can we hone in on the *real* answers hiding behind the wall of illusion that separates us from the vast intelligence of the Universe. Our questions then become cracks in the façade of untruth. If we keep asking and listening, the wall must begin to break apart.

The "Q" in B ☰ Q O M I N G also symbolizes the intersection between the masculine and feminine energies, which create the vast playground of polarity, or opposites, upon which reality itself depends.

These polarities express themselves upon the canvas of up and down, right and left, love and fear, doing and being, hot and cold, and life and death.

Without its signature tail, the Q remains an O—a feminine symbol of the infinite, the circle of life. But when the masculine line injects linear form into this infinite loop, anchoring it with stability and direction, it blossoms and grows. Therefore, in our eyes, the letter Q symbolically holds the source frequency of life itself.

We humans are an extension of nature's intelligent design, even though most of us have forgotten that intrinsic connection. When we take the vast canvas of our own life experience and begin to deliberately apply ourselves to our soul's growth—we blossom. Therefore, **the path of B Ξ Q O M I N G is a path of integration**. Of making whole that which has been split. Of bringing into balance that which has been lopsided. Of unifying our energies to come into our full being.

The EQ in B Ξ Q O M I N G also speaks to the power of emotional intelligence, which is a foundational component of the frame-work we will share with you in this book. Our emotions are master teachers, albeit forgotten ones, and we will explore them and their role in great depth throughout this journey.

Joseph Campbell describes bliss as "any feeling fully felt"—and we feel that this simple statement contains the key that can crack the code to all of life. Practicing non-resistance to whatever feelings are arising in the moment, no matter how unpleasant they may appear to be, liberates us from the purgatory of preference and allows us to tap into the realm of simply *experiencing* the "energy in motion," which is what emotion actually is.

Now let us define a few more unique terms we will be using consistently throughout this journey of B Ξ Q O M I N G.

Your Truest Truth

Fully devoting yourself to B Ξ Q O M I N G is about finding what we call your Truest Truth and following it. This Truest Truth we speak of is a form of truth that exists in harmony with the Universe and Love's intelligence, beyond the static of patterned behaviors, emotional turbulence, and even individual preference. It is in service to something greater, something beyond logic and reason. It requires learning how to discern between the various forms of truth one can experience in any given moment and realizing that when we get fixed on one version of what we think the truth is and begin defending it, we lose contact with the very thing that informs our Truest Truth in every moment anew: *Love.*

KNOWING

To sift through all the noise to get to our Truest Truth, we must continually be willing to relinquish the intellectual knowing of the mind and tap into the KNOWING that sits deep in the ancient wisdom of our bones and in our hearts.

Just as the word **gnosis** describes mystical or esoteric knowledge based on direct participation with the divine, our definition of KNOWING (in all caps) exists beyond the intellectual "knowing" that comes from the acquired knowledge of scholarly study and personal experience—all of which is constantly shapeshifting and being debunked and reframed or redefined. As Sadhguru says: "What we call knowledge refers to frozen, accumulated memory. KNOWING, on the other hand, is a dynamic process; it is living wisdom, not dead information."

KNOWING is an innate and intimate remembrance of your own, ancient intelligence, and is steadfast in a conviction that exists beyond all external knowledge. It is irrefutable, and, often, inexplicable.

The Choiceless Choice

The Choiceless Choice is a paradox, in that it is a choice that you make intentionally but that simultaneously feels like you don't have a choice. It's the sensation of your path choosing itself through you, guided by something greater than yourself. When you're making a Choiceless Choice, you're *allowing what wants to happen*, beyond what you think your personal preferences are.

Unfuckwithable

When we've developed and refined our emotional intelligence (EQ) to the point where we are predominantly *responding* versus *reacting* to triggers; when we've learned to listen beyond the chatter of the mind and discern between knowing and KNOWING; when we've made living in alignment with our Truest Truth our highest priority—that is when we begin to touch the realm of B☰QOMING Unfuckwithable, which we define as: *the ability to embody openhearted acceptance of What Is, no matter the circumstances.*

Don't worry about trying to memorize these distinctions. Through the true stories of our B Ξ Q O M I N G, you will receive many reference points with which to understand them, and we will use them over and over again in their right context.

You may even find yourself spontaneously beginning to integrate these words into your own vocabulary because they provide nuances that our general definitions of truth, knowing, and becoming simply don't encompass.

Trust that simply receiving the living template of our own lived experiences will do a lot of the work for you.

HOW TO USE THIS BOOK

Even if you never walk the path of B Ξ Q O M I N G through the avenues of committed partnership or plant medicine, this book will give you plenty of tools, references, examples, and modalities to forge your own unique path.

And while there is simply no right or wrong way to B Ξ Q O M Ξ, there are distinct patterns that have emerged through our continued work in this arena, which have allowed us to identify many of the universal themes of the process and illuminate them with awareness.

In every chapter, we are going to show you uncensored examples of how these patterns manifested in our real lives. Our intention in doing so is to provide as much value as possible through using ourselves as case studies on the journey of B Ξ Q O M I N G, for as we've learned, the same themes emerge time and time again within the collective of our human family. After each personal story we share, we will distill the main takeaways for you to integrate into your own life. Then you will have the opportunity to answer relevant questions designed to activate your own B Ξ Q O M I N G.

We recommend that on your first read-through you have a journal handy so you can answer the questions right away while the information is fresh.

To dive deeper, we have compiled various resources, such as guided meditations and other transformational content, which you can access at *www. B Ξ Q O M I N G.me/tools*.

Also, at the end of the audio version of this book you will find juicy bonus interviews with many of the real-life characters that you will meet in the coming pages.

Many of our digital offerings are based on a Free Will Investment model, meaning you pick your own financial contribution based entirely on your level of inspiration to invest in your own B Ξ Q O M I N G process. All profits will go to our non-profit, *B Ξ Q O M I N G Stewards of Society*, which in turn funds heart-centered people and projects to make the world a more beautiful and compassionate place.

If the time is right and your soul is ripe for evolution, you will carve out the necessary time to answer the questions in this book and feel inspired and energized as you do the accompanying exercises.

If you're just skimming these pages, we recommend coming back when you feel a shift into being truly present with this journey. (Usually that shift will feel like an internal opening, or a soft knocking from within that gets louder over time, inviting you to peel the layers back and look deeper at yourself, your life, and your reality with greater and greater urgency.)

If that internal *KNOWING* of your readiness to strip, crack, shed, break, stretch, and expand into a new version of yourself isn't fully available to you yet, that's okay. Maybe it isn't the right time. We simply invite you to approach this path wholeheartedly. To be open to what we have to share, and to engage with it fully.

At the end of the day, only you can decide how deeply you will let yourself be penetrated by the words on these pages. You could plow through this entire book, extract a few valuable nuggets, and then forget all about it and go back to your default setting.

Or this book could be the doorway into a radical new version of who you never dared imagine you could be.

We can point you to the threshold, but only you can choose to cross over.

PART 1

STRIPPED AWAKE

1

WHAT'S IT GOING TO TAKE?

"Life does not accommodate you, it shatters
you. It is meant to, and it couldn't do it
better. Every seed destroys its container
or else there would be no fruition."

—Florida Scott-Maxwell

WELCOME TO ROCK BOTTOM

Bee: The pressure is too much to handle. I am cracking. Losing it. I need to get out. To run away from my reality.

I can't do this.

I mumble something about having a meeting to one of the co-founders of our company, who also happens to be my best friend—and my father. Then I leave the building. I make a beeline for my car, get behind the wheel, and start driving. Where, I don't know. I can't go home. Home isn't a safe place, because home is where my guilt is amplified. I choose the open road instead.

With no destination, I drive for hours, sobbing.

How did I get here? How could a 35-year-old, healthy man from loving immigrant parents, with two beautiful kids, a loyal wife, and a self-built family business generating $200MM in annual revenue feel *anything* but confident and fulfilled?

The hard truth is, confident and fulfilled is the opposite of how I feel. I am wracked with insecurity and guilt. I feel trapped by a reality of my own design. Over the last few years, obligations I've chosen to carry have become so debilitating that I have literally broken my back from the weight. Still plagued by the chronic pain from a dirt bike accident that crushed my L1–L5 vertebrae two years ago, I realize—my extreme dirt biking phase was just another attempt to mask my pain with adrenaline. Another attempt to escape.

But I can't escape now. I'm in too deep. And I know that I also can't blame anyone or anything outside of me. I'm doing this to myself. I'm my own worst enemy. Fear has me in its vice grip, and I'm paralyzed—unable to regain control of my life, just like I couldn't regain control of the bike when I failed to clear the double on that track and got slammed into the ground. Pushing myself to the extreme almost killed me that day.

And, truthfully, I have moments where I wish it did.

As I hurtle down the Southern California freeway toward nowhere, I think about my beloved parents, who fled Cuba in the 1960s with nothing but the shirts on their back, eating Saltines on their honeymoon and yet too proud to accept welfare, so eager were they to get on their feet and live the American dream.

Here I am, doing just that. And the American dream has failed me.

I think back to the day my dad called me when I was on the verge of graduating from the University of San Diego with a hard-earned business degree and a blank slate as my future. I could hear the fear in his voice as he confessed that he was on the verge of bankruptcy and wanted to start a new business venture—with me as a partner.

"A Hispanic grocery store, Dad?" Twenty-three-year-old me said, standing at the kitchen counter in my boxer shorts, chomping on a salad bowl-sized serving of Frosted Flakes and Fruity Pebbles cereal. "We don't know the first thing about that kind of business."

"Listen to me," he replied. The desperation in his voice made me lower my spoon. This is serious. "We have to do this for the family. I need your help."

He was asking me, but he wasn't really asking. And he didn't have to. It was a given that I would show up for the family. It's just how we were wired. Loyal to the bone. So I forfeited my secret dreams to attend law school and stepped in.

That was my first real experience of the Choiceless Choice. And it terrified me.

Even though nothing about starting a Hispanic grocery store business excited me, I threw myself headfirst into the challenge. Our first store was a run-down Market Basket from the 1950s with a lease so shitty, our lawyer advised my dad not to sign it. Dad did anyway. Stubborn motherfucker. The place was a dump. Hundreds of pigeons were living in the rafters. My father, brother, and I helped with all the hands-on construction and even dug the trenches for the plumbing. We didn't know the first thing about plumbing. We'd come home so filthy my mom made us strip down to our underwear before entering the house.

Getting the business off the ground took my parents' entire life savings. They sold their ranch and their garment factory, refinanced our house, borrowed $50,000 from my grandparents, and maxed out every credit card to make it happen. "I'd rather sell oranges on the side of the road than work for someone else," my father once told me. Because of the terrible lease, we had five years to save up enough money to buy the building or the landlord could kick us out and we would lose everything. Sinking wasn't an option. We had to swim.

Fear is a powerful force of nature. It can create the kind of pressure that moves mountains. But eventually, it runs out of steam and, like mold, destroys the very thing it created from the inside out.

As I ignore the many incoming texts and calls from all the people depending on my direction, I am paralyzed by the realization that being driven by fear for so long has completely burnt me out. Not only that—I am living a version of myself that I was always terrified of becoming.

And of course I am. Growing up, my only reference point for what being a man is supposed to look like was my father: working his ass off in a profession he hated, miserable, and trapped by his own fear of failure.

Don't get me wrong—my father is a legend, a man whom I deeply love and respect, a man who can light up a room with his laugh and talk to anyone about anything, a man who sacrifices everything for his family and always puts them first. But he is also a man who allows fear to run his life—and that fear will eventually cost him his life.

Right now, I am following in his footsteps.

A light pops up on the dash, alerting me that my tank is close to empty. I'm literally and metaphorically running on fumes, driven by a deep fear of failing as a man. Failing as a provider. Failing as a husband.

I have two kids, Gysel, age six, and Steel, age one, who is about to be diagnosed with autism. I have a devoted wife, Grisel, who I barely knew when we got married and still barely know. We are—at our core—not compatible, and I have never fully let her in. The monster family business that has, fueled by the blood, sweat, and tears of 80–90-hour work weeks, become wildly successful and allowed me to fall in love with being an entrepreneur is now being threatened by a tanking economy and ever-increasing competition.

On top of that, I have no faith, no religion, no compass to guide me through this valley of fear, to liberate me from the prison of my own mind.

Boo hoo, the voice in my head berates me. *Here you are, with a beautiful family, money in the bank, fantasizing about being dead. You have no right to feel this way.*

I drive, and I am alone. Feeling utterly trapped in every area of my life.

Welcome to my rock bottom.

Azrya: The tequila runs through my veins, thick like molten honey. I am no longer in charge of my body; it's making decisions for me now, and I feel reckless and out of control as I dance and sway to the music in the night club, where I also happen to work. Tonight is my night off, but I came here because I can drink for free, and when you're a 21-year-old struggling actress in Hollywood who lives on an air mattress from Target in an unfurnished room off of Craigslist and hustles for tips, you don't say no to anything free— especially $20 cocktails.

Amidst the sea of people, I see a familiar face. A handsome face of an actor I met once before at an audition, during which there was an undeniable chemistry between us. Mind you, I'm fresh off the boat from Germany, where I spent my last five years in two committed, monogamous relationships, both of which ended in devastating heartbreak. Playing the part of a wild, give-no-fucks chick that can have a one-night stand with a total stranger just because she feels like it sounds pretty fucking liberating right now, compared to all the emotional drama I'm used to.

Sober, my boundaries and inhibitions would never let me play that part, but now, eight tequila shots deep, I am all courage and no boundaries. I'm also the sloppy version of me, of course, but that doesn't seem to bother the man as I take him by the hand and start heading for the exit. It's on.

Next thing I know, we're in the backseat of my $600, 1986 Lincoln town car and he's inside of me. I am so numb I can barely feel a thing. All the rocking makes me nauseous. As soon as it's over, I open the car door and puke onto the sidewalk below.

I wipe the vomit off of my chin, not feeling quite as liberated as I thought I would.

Pretending to be way less drunk than I am, I offer to drive him to his car.

"Are you sure?" he asks. He's not a bad guy, just a Hollywood kid chasing the shiny dream like all of us. "For sure," I assure him. "I got this!"

By the time I drop him off, I have no idea what part of town I'm in. I don't have a smartphone, so I decide to just pick a direction and figure it out. I've only lived in LA for six months, but I'm sure I'll recognize a street sign somewhere.

I can't remember when I blacked out, but it was somewhere in Beverly Hills around 4 a.m. And when I come to, the first thing I feel is confused. *Am I dreaming?*

Torrents of water cascade onto my cracked windshield. The contents of my spilled purse are swimming in more water that is rising up to my knees from the ground. Dazed, I look down at myself. A few droplets of blood adorn my cleavage. I flip the visor down to see myself. Red-rimmed eyes. A busted lip. No, I'm not dreaming. I just got *stripped awake*.

Behind me, blue and red cop car lights flash. I'm not alone anymore.

I try to get out of the car, but the handle is jammed. Later, I learn in addition to the fire hydrant that I slammed into going about 50 mph, I also toppled a telephone pole, which is now blocking my door. I awkwardly climb out on the passenger side.

The cop approaching me has a kind face.

"What happened?" he asks, genuinely amazed at the mess I made.

I shrug. "I don't know," I say. Then I climb into the ambulance, get seven stitches in my lip, and am told that my blood alcohol content is so high, I should definitely be going to jail. Instead, the cops take pity on me and I get a free pass to go home instead. The rest will figure itself out in court.

As I sit in the back of the cab, watching the sun rise over the City of Angels, I feel a profound sensation expand inside of me. It is the still flame of awareness, burning away the unconsciousness that almost just cost me my life. It's the moment where I realize that shrugging and saying "I don't know" is not who I am supposed to be.

Quietly and humbly, in the back of that cab, I decide to take the steering wheel of my life back into my own hands.

No, this is not my ultimate awakening moment. That moment doesn't come for another six years. But it's a start. A glimpse of remembering that life is precious, fleetingly precious. It is a course correction, a divine intervention, a gift from the universe to force me to stop pretending that I am not powerful. To force me to look at where I am running from myself, numbing myself, dishonoring myself. Blindly driven by a distorted fantasy of what it means to be wild, empowered, and free. Wasting myself by trying to fill myself with all the wrong things.

What am I trying to fill?
The answers come from inside me.
A deep longing in my heart of hearts.
A yearning to matter.
To understand why I am here.
To feel whole. To come home. To be alive.
To love.

I don't know it at the time, but I have just said yes to my
B≡ǪOMING.

B≡ǪOMING OPEN

We: *Kintsugi* is the Japanese art of putting broken pottery pieces
back together with gold lacquer—built on the idea that by embracing flaws and imperfections, you can create an even stronger, more
beautiful piece of art.

In order for that beautification process to occur, though, the pottery has to break.

This is what the journey of B≡ǪOMING demands of anyone
stepping on this path.

There's a cracking that's occurring within all of us that is irrefutable. A part of you KNOWS this, and feels the ever-increasing
intensity of the drumbeat inviting you to B≡ǪOM≡ an active
participant in the larger, evolutionary process on Earth that is
reaching its fever pitch.

Whether we choose to actively acknowledge it or not, *it's happening*. The world is rapidly shapeshifting before our very eyes, and
the raw force of evolution doesn't give a fuck about our 401(k)
comfort zones.

You Picked Up This Book for a Reason

Maybe you are actively seeking expansion and have been on your personal development path for a while, but something is still missing. Perhaps you've found yourself scrolling your newsfeed, watching the crescendo of recent global events, and are wondering *"WTF is actually going on in the world right now?"* Maybe you're feeling a stir to create more meaning in your day-to-day experience of reality. To be of greater contribution, to be fueled by purpose, to make an impact.

Perhaps you are restless, anxious, or quietly stirring with a frustration that won't quit. Or, perhaps you are feeling trapped— in a marriage, in a career, in your own mental chatter and stress responses—haunted by the possibility that the true richness of life is somehow slipping through your fingers like sand.

Maybe the success you've sacrificed so much to achieve has lost some of its allure, and thrill has turned to routine. And perhaps you rationalize all of this by convincing yourself that everything is *just fine*. You've ticked all the boxes; you should feel like you've won, right?

What if you don't feel that much at all?

No matter what led you to this book, here's our message to you:

You're not trapped.
You haven't failed.

You're not too late.
Nothing is wrong with you.

You are simply dormant. The fully expressed genius of your unique design has not come online yet. You may have caught glimpses of it, maybe even felt it for phases, but you haven't embodied it or landed in it fully. It hasn't become your default— your new normal.

That's because you haven't claimed it yet. You are still hiding from it. But here's a tip: you can't hide forever, and it's pointless to keep trying. Your genius is relentless in its pursuit of you. It will not give up until you stop and listen to what it has in store for you. And yes, we're speaking to the part of you that already knows this. You might not consciously or intellectually remember it yet, but you've been waiting for this activation, and it's been waiting for you.

Waiting to reveal to you *everything you didn't know you wanted.*

The Choice Is Yours

It's hard to say where the journey of B≡QOMING truly starts. When we asked ourselves this question while reviewing our personal lives, we traced it back to the rock bottom stories you just read. These were the pivotal turning point moments for us that created that first crack in the façade of our realities and forced us to take a long, hard look at how out of alignment with our Truest Truth we really were.

The journey of B≡QOMING doesn't have to be catalyzed by such intense and dramatic rock-bottom moments. Some people genuinely just wake up one day and feel a sudden inspiration to change their entire lives, without anything in their external reality overtly prompting them to do so. But this is not the case for most.

Why does life jar us in such painful ways?

Because we have been deeply conditioned to avoid pain, and B≡QOMING (just like childbirth) is going to include pain in some way, shape, or form.

Usually, that pain is emotional pain—the kind we are least equipped to navigate. Think about it. We spend years sitting in classrooms, learning algebra and memorizing war dates, while our emotional intelligence training falls by the wayside. Where are the tools to embrace our depression, our rage, our resentment? Why are we taught to be "good girls" and "good boys" who politely smile and say "I'm fine," when really what we want to say is *"I'm fucking confused and hurt right now!"*

Well, here's one possible explanation. Try it on for size:

Life, for human beings, up until this point, has largely been focused on physical survival, and so there hasn't been a lot of room for cultivating emotional well-being. When our recent ancestors had to spend countless hours tilling hard soil in the hopes of making it through winter, saying "Meh, I don't *feel* like it today" would have been preposterous. That necessity of survival, coupled with the systemic oppression of all things feminine for thousands of years, has led to our feelings being mostly suppressed, rejected, and denied. This suppression mechanism is deeply ingrained in our DNA.

We are biologically hardwired to go to great lengths to pretend that we're fine. We've gotten so good at convincing others, we've almost convinced ourselves. But this suppression has come at a cost, for emotions are energy, and as we know, energy can never be created nor destroyed, only changed in form.

So what happens when billions of people are carrying all of this unconscious, pent-up, accumulated darkness from untouched emotions around in their hearts, bodies, and minds? It's like a ticking time bomb.

Eventually, the pressure is too great and the pot boils over.

Welcome to the current shit show that's going down on planet Earth.

What we're seeing in the collective right now is a necessary purge of all the unprocessed emotional material that we've been passing down from one generation to the next, at the root of which is pure fear. Much of this material exists in our subconscious, which is why it's often called the shadow. Whether it's COVID-19, Black Lives Matter, or Me Too, we are being confronted with a collective that is being stripped awake, unable to pretend like everything is "just fine" any longer.

Because this purge process is deeply uncomfortable and disturbing and we really have no clue how to handle it, the knee-jerk reaction is often to try and keep the lid on with even greater force. To cling to the status quo, the "way things were," and just ignore the increasingly urgent whispers from our own inner voice to meet the B Ξ Q O MI N G process head on. You can see why Trump's slogan "Make America Great Again" was such a success. It spoke directly to the part of us that yearns for things to just feel wholesome again. It hurts to acknowledge that this wholesomeness was largely a fairy tale and never actually the whole truth. Pandemics, slave labor, and sexual exploitation have been a prominent part of our human history for thousands of years, and the devastating impact of these energies on our emotional bodies is finally ready to be expressed and transmuted into a much healthier expression of humanity. This is a massive endeavor and will require each and every single one of us to play our part.

As we've experienced, resistance to our own evolution is futile and sometimes even dangerous. If you are resisting your own darkness, your own wounding, your own personalized call to be an active participant in the full expression of your soul, sooner or later, life will confront you in a way that gives you no choice but to wake up.

For Benjamin, it took reaching the pinnacle of traditional, material "success" and wishing he was dead. For Azrya, it took a head-on collision with a Beverly Hills fire hydrant to snap her to attention.

What will it be for you? A diagnosis? An accident? A divorce? Seeing your children struggling with the same core wounds you do? Getting everything you ever desired and still feeling a dull ache on the inside? Will you be like us and ignore the subtle whispers of your Truest Truth until the universe punches you in the face—or are you going to choose to listen, act now, and let this be the beginning of your journey?

It doesn't have to be hard. Reading this book can be enough to catalyze your BEQOMING. We designed it that way.

The choice is, always has been, and always will be yours.

INVITATION #1:

- Take inventory of your current life circumstances. How do you feel about where you're at right now?

- Are you resisting or embracing your genius? Elaborate.

- Are you aware of any unprocessed emotional material that may be blocking you from BEQOMING who you were designed to be? Describe.

- Are you experiencing a call to action from the universe? Is there a cracking open occurring or wanting to occur in your framework of reality? If so, how has this come into your awareness, and why do you think it's happening?

2

YOU SIGNED UP FOR THIS

> "It's like your childhood wounds
> have constructed a revolving door of
> reality you cannot seem to exit."
>
> —Londin Angel Winters

LEARNING MASTER LESSONS

Bee: I am sitting in the driver's seat next to my girlfriend Olga. We are on our way to a numerology reading. Not long ago, I didn't even know that numerology existed, much less that I'd be the kind of person who would pay money for such a thing. But here I am. My thirst to optimize myself is what made me say yes to something I would have written off as totally "woo-woo" not long ago. Having just sold my business and gotten a divorce, I'm looking for direction, guidance, and clarity on what's next for me. I am calling in answers.

The woman conducting the reading is well known and respected in her esoteric circles. I wouldn't be going to her if her predictions hadn't proven to be spot-on for several of Olga's friends. She's booked out months in advance, which further legitimizes her and allows me to suspend my skepticism.

Sitting in front of her now, she asks for my birth information, then calculates my fate.

"You are destined to be a master teacher," she says, matter-of-fact.

My ego likes this news. *Fuck yeah.* Since I was 16, I've always longed to share something significant with the world. Maybe this woman can tell me how to unlock that part of me; maybe she can help me find my real purpose. It's about time. I'm already 40 years old. I know how to make money, but I have no idea how to leave a legacy of true impact.

I lean in closer.

"The challenge is," she continues, "to become a master teacher, you will have to learn master lessons."

Squinting at the numerology calculations, she continues.

"You will be learning master lessons for the next seven years. Your purpose won't reveal itself until you are 47. Then things will click into place and you will receive the clarity you seek." She looks up.

What did you just say, lady!?

I feel immediate contraction in my body. Impatience. Frustration. Disappointment. I don't like this prediction I've just paid good money for, not one bit. Having just devoted 15 years to working my ass off so I could provide for my family, seven years of learning feels like an eternity. Her words land in my body like a prison sentence.

As I exit the building after the session, the hot summer air feels almost suffocating. I am leaving with more uncertainty than I came with. I'm annoyed with myself for having gone in the first place. I want to forget what she said, to write it off as bullshit, but I can't unhear her words. Somewhere deep inside me, I KNOW she has spoken the truth. I KNOW she is talking about me B Ξ Q O M I N G the man I aspire to be.

At the time of that reading, I did not yet view life as intelligent and the universe as benevolent. I lived in a random universe in which things only happened if you made them happen. Results were created by exerting force over matter, by learning to harness the power of will, hard work, and discipline. The idea that my soul was enrolled in a cosmic curriculum designed to mold and shape me into the highest expression of myself was foreign and far-fetched.

Not anymore.

If you Google the word "soul," the first definition you'll find is: "The spiritual or immaterial part of a human being or animal, regarded as immortal."

Using the seven years of master lessons as an example, the way I understand it is this: My soul—the part of me that exists beyond this physical dimension of time and space and therefore has a kind of zoomed-out lens on reality—came here to learn very specific lessons in this lifetime. These lessons are available to be learned within the everyday reality of my human experiences, which make up the curriculum that my soul is enrolled in.

Azrya and I often talk about the concept of destiny. We don't buy into fate as a fixed thing that we have no choice but to helplessly submit to. It's not so black and white for us. Rather, we believe there's a sweet spot where fate and free will intersect.

Just like when I was getting my pilot's license and the aviation curriculum adjusted to my pace, so does the universe mirror back to me my willingness and readiness to expand, which I get to determine with my own free will. In the pilot license example, the more committed, focused, and optimistic I was about advancing, the faster the next lesson came, until five months later, I could legally fly.

Had I let fear, doubt, or indifference interfere, it may have taken me three times as long to get in the air, if I made it at all. With my free will, I could have even chosen to give up entirely and just quit, but while I may have never been able to call myself a pilot, the universe would have found some new expression of that exact same emotional curriculum to confront me with instead because, as I've come to trust, the universe wants me to evolve, and the best way it can get me to do that is to systematically and relentlessly confront me with all of my own perceived limitations and deepest fears.

When Azrya asked me how I felt about that numerology prediction now that I was on the other side of the seven years of master lessons, many of which were grueling, I simply said: "It couldn't have been any other way."

In hindsight, so much of my soul curriculum has been and continues to be about trust. Trust in myself to be enough, and trust that the universe's plan for me isn't going to lead me straight off a cliff. Because, damn—it sure as hell has come close, more than a few times.

We call the challenging aspects of this course material "shadow work."

From what Azrya and I can tell, based on the B Ξ Q O MI N G process we facilitate for individuals, soul curriculum starts the moment we are born and often orchestrates pivotal moments during childhood where the overarching theme for the curriculum is revealed—usually through the form of some traumatic event.

Trauma can be extreme, or it can be subtle. While I never suffered physical abuse during childhood, beyond being occasionally hit with a belt by my otherwise loving father, the emotional pain that I experienced in school was excruciating and left a lasting scar. With learning disabilities so severe I could barely read a simple sentence out loud without crippling anxiety, school was a constant reflection of my shortcomings and drilled into me over and over again the deep-rooted belief that I was incompetent, if not downright stupid.

Then came Little League.

The Broken-Hearted Little Boy

"Your son's got real potential," the coach says to my father on the phone. "We know he's only 10, but he had a good try-out, and we'd like to offer him a spot on the advanced team. See how he does with the 13-year-olds. What do you say?"

Of course, my dad agrees. He doesn't have the awareness to realize that the three-year gap is setting his son up for the ultimate inferiority complex. He's just proud that I got picked.

I'm a great athlete and love to play, but sure enough, being the smallest kid on the team is devastating to my self-esteem. I can't hit the ball; the pitches are too fast. No matter how hard I try, I can't compete. The feeling of being incompetent and not enough that I deal with every day in my academics has followed me into sports, the one place I used to feel confident.

One day it gets so bad, I abandon the field mid-game and go looking for my dad in the bleachers. Sobbing and mortified, I beg him to take me out of the game and let me go home. My dad makes the choice he thinks is the most loving one. The alpha male, tough love choice. "Get back out there, son," he commands. My dad is my universe at that time, and the universe just proved itself to be ruthless. My heart, trusting in my dad to support me and love me, to see my pain and hold me close, has just been broken.

That deep trust breach within myself and the universe follows me into high school, then college. Without asking my parents, I decide at age 15 that I'm done with the private all-boys school that I hate and enroll myself in the local public school, where the curriculum is a lot less demanding and cheating is a lot easier. Cheating is my saving grace.

With my grades being so poor, I can't apply to any universities initially, so I begin my higher education in community college, where I discover business and find my groove. I realize that I like money. Money inspires me. I get accepted to the University of San Diego the following year to get a degree in business. Upon hearing this, my mother reveals a secret that causes my father to lose his shit. Without his knowing, she's been saving money for my college education. Even as we were on the verge of bankruptcy and my father was slaving away on his knees, she stood her ground so that I could have a future.

Now, with tremendous gratitude in my heart for her iron-clad ovaries, I begin my academic life at USD with my tuition paid for in full. Still, I don't feel like I belong. I feel like an imposter. Yeah, I'm good with numbers and have a knack for entrepreneurial thinking, but I still can barely read out loud. Violence doesn't scare me— words on the page do.

These insecurities show up in my relationships as well, although I deny them and put on masks to keep my composure. I find myself jealous, even though my girlfriend has given me no reason to be. On the outside, I am a tough, confident motherfucker and finally getting good grades. On the inside, the little boy that couldn't hit the ball and can't read is still trembling.

That little boy follows me into my career. At its peak, our family Hispanic grocery store business has 1,800 employees, 12 locations, a 300,000 square foot warehouse and is grossing over $200MM in annual revenue, but it's not enough to calm his trembles or soothe his cries. If anything, it makes him more nervous, wondering if he just got lucky and it's all going to crash and burn around him once the world realizes that he's not as competent as everyone thinks he is.

My father and I grow extremely close as we build the business together. His faith gives me the courage to step into shoes that I don't believe I can fill. He treats me as an equal, and we become best friends and mentors to each other.

Nine years into our venture, an investment banker tells us we can get somewhere from $80–130MM for the business.

I do the math. We are about to open two new locations, and I'm convinced they will crush it. I calculate that if we wait just another six months to sell, we can add another $20MM to the sales price. This is a choice point, a pop quiz from the universe.

I tell my dad, "I think we should wait." He agrees.

Then, the competition unexpectedly expands into many of the areas we are doing business. The economy gets hit hard. Those six months turn into three of the hardest years of my life.

In the end, we sell the business for a third of what we could have, had we let it be *enough*.

In hindsight, it wasn't really me who made that decision to hold off on selling. At first I thought it was just plain old greed—but now that I have the context of soul curriculum, I realize it was the trembling little boy inside that had forgotten how to trust. Who didn't believe he was enough and therefore needed more and more external evidence to prove his worth. He didn't know how to be satisfied with his accomplishments, no matter how impressive they may have appeared to everyone else.

I am reminded of a cartoon of a dog holding a bone in his mouth, who peers over the edge of a pond and sees in the reflection a dog holding a bone in his mouth. Unaware that what he sees is an illusion, he goes to snatch the bone, and in doing so, loses the one he already has.

My soul curriculum forced me to see where I had become that dog. The misbelief that achieving more externally would help me feel whole internally continued to shape my experience of reality, even after we sold the business and redeployed the money into real estate and other investments with great success.

The more successful I became, the more the memory of the trembling little boy began to fade, but every now and then, especially when I was in a room full of impressive CEOs or waking up next to a drop-dead gorgeous woman I had met at a bar the night before, he would let me know that he was still in there, following me. Reminding me that there was a very real possibility that all of my achievements were just a fluke. And that I could be, in fact, still just cheating my way through life, hoping not to get caught.

A Broken Promise

Azrya: It's a warm summer afternoon in Hamburg, Germany, and I hear my grandmother calling from the balcony for me to come in and have "Kaffee und Kuchen"—which means coffee and cake time. I'm only six years old, so I don't participate in the coffee part, but the promise of cake is motivation enough to get me off the lawn, where I've been in deep communion with the daisies and grasses, basking in the delicious sensation of the Earth's gentle embrace. Having just moved here from New York, this lawn, these scents, this sky feels like a new universe to me, and I'm still taking it all in.

Once inside the small condo, I find my beloved grandmother— whom I call Mutzi—setting the table with her special china.

"Go wash your hands," she says in German. As I trot off to the bathroom with a bounce in my step, a loud, disturbing sound interrupts the tranquility of my six-year-old heart. It's coming from outside and stops me in my tracks. I follow the sound to the open balcony door and step outside. Standing on my tippy toes to peer over the edge of the railing, I recoil in horror when I discover the source of the sound.

It's a lawn mower, and it's ruthlessly decapitating all of my brand-new daisy friends.

Instantly, tears gush down my face as I watch the blades annihilate the soft bed of grass that had just held me so lovingly a mere five minutes ago. Paralyzed and outraged, I stand and watch the massacre take place, utterly helpless. It's like I am the lawn, and the machine is obliviously mowing my vital organs apart as if it were the most normal thing in the world.

As I grow up, I realize mowing a lawn is considered normal.

Feeling the lawn as deeply as I do is not.

Hypersensitive empaths don't function well in a disconnected modern world. Thankfully, Mutzi holds me in a protective bubble for the next four years while my mother travels for a lot of that time. This bubble allows me to preserve my innocence for as long as possible, but eventually, the force field of her love isn't strong enough.

One day, my mother comes over with news. When she sweeps in, I can feel the unspoken tension between her and Mutzi, and it makes my little body feel like it's being split in two.

"I've decided we're moving back to New York," my mother announces. Mutzi's face drains of color. She knows that by "we," she means me (my name is Melinda at the time), and my mom. Mutzi is too old to make the move between continents again. Hamburg is her original home, the place she survived World War II. She needs to stay here and live out her days.

Except she wasn't planning to do it without me. And the truth is, I've become her sole purpose in life. With very little family and few friends, her reality without me is empty. Even though I'm only 10, I intuitively understand how much she needs me. As we take our daily walk, autumn leaves crunching beneath our boots, I hold her by the hand, feeling a deep desperation seep from her weathered skin into mine. That damn empathy again.

"Melinda," she says, her voice seeped in pain. "I want you to stay with me, and I think you want to stay too. Will you tell your mother that you don't want to go to New York with her?" Her voice is pleading. I can't say no.

"Of course, Mutzi," I assure her, squeezing her hand. "I promise."

At the same time, I also sense that my mother's decision is final, and I, as a sensitive 10-year-old, don't have the power to change her mind. I end up not even trying. It doesn't feel true to resist this change that life is pulling me toward. I surrender to the flow, a practice that defines me to this day.

Sure enough, not long after making a promise I was never equipped to keep, I pack everything that can fit into one duffel bag and head to the airport with my mother to start a new life, yet again. I am excited to be closer to my father, who is a musicology professor at Harvard and who I barely remember. My parents never married. He left when I was one.

At the same time, the excitement of my new life is tainted by a deep-seated guilt around abandoning my beloved Mutzi. Every summer I go to visit her, I feel the wound of betrayal creating a splinter of disconnection between us. Just like I felt the daisies being decapitated, I can feel her isolation and despair seeping from the carpets and walls of the condo I used to call home. I decide with the utmost conviction that it's all my fault. That if I had been able to keep my word, she would not have had to suffer the agony of having the light extinguished from her life.

Over the next five years, Mutzi goes almost completely blind, and the almost 4,000 miles between us as well as my blooming adolescence and ever-increasing independence has created an irreparable distance between us. My summer vacation visits feel more and more strained. I can sense her resenting me. The more guilty I feel, the more I retreat. Not just from her, but from the magic of life itself. My empathic connection to the plant and animal world isn't considered cool in my new school, and I'm quickly labeled "the weird German girl." I feel like an outcast. I try really hard to stop caring so damn much and to just be cool. I get pretty good at playing the part. Wearing a mask is a lot of work, though, so I am constantly looking for validation from others that I'm doing a good job.

One day, when I am 15, I come home from school to find my mother waiting for me with more news.

"Mutzi is dying," she says.

We board a plane, and I witness my beloved grandmother deteriorate in her own bed, unable to penetrate the invisible walls that separate us now. By the time she crosses over, I feel relieved; the guilt has been all consuming. I blame myself for all of her suffering and subconsciously make her death mean that getting too close to me must be dangerous. I develop a deep fear of being depended on by anyone, which further fuels my fierce attachment to independence.

Truth is, I don't trust myself to keep a promise. I don't trust myself to stay.

At this stage of my journey, I have no awareness of how deep-rooted belief systems shape and mold reality. The belief that getting too close to me is dangerous and hurts the people I love is confirmed over and over again through leaving behind various friendships as my mother and I continue moving around. The heartbreaking goodbyes become a common theme in my soul curriculum, made tangible in my emotional body through the feeling of intense guilt and betrayal.

Because my empathy is so high, the agony I cause repeatedly in others when I inevitably leave rips me apart from the inside to the point where I can't cope. I don't have the tools to navigate the intensity of these emotions, so my body tries to protect itself by suppressing and numbing. By the time I'm 17, now living in Germany again after having lived in 14 different places, I am so numb that cutting myself is the only way I can feel something.

Poetry written in blood ensues. My independence has evolved into rebelliousness. I am committed to giving as few fucks as possible, but the harder I try to reject my true empathic nature, the more miserable I become.

It takes a lot of energy to constantly try and escape the truth of who you are.

Acting becomes my safe haven. On the stage or in front of the camera, I can hide behind a character who gives me permission to feel all the things I don't dare feel in my real life. At age 19, I decide to study acting instead of going to college—it's the only career path that excites me. When I break up with my boyfriend of three years, he is in such despair that he locks himself in the bathroom with a butcher knife while I'm pounding on the door weeping, calling 911. This experience becomes yet another confirmation of how dangerous I am to those I love. The guilt intensifies.

Upon my graduation from acting school, I follow the call to Hollywood, once again leaving heartbreak in my wake as I ungracefully exit my latest relationship to board a plane and follow my truth.

I glorify the idea of being a single girl who casually dates. *That will be safer because we won't catch feelings, right?*

Wrong. My dating life in LA is miserable, filled with drama and resentment from men who instantly pile expectations onto me and give me their hearts, even though I never asked for them. I decide it's not worth it, and—after my rock-bottom DUI moment, which was my first and last one-night stand—I focus all of my energy on my career instead. But acting is a profession of feeling, and all the numbing has taken its toll. I find it challenging to surrender to the character's circumstances, and I start getting in my own way. My auditions suffer, so I try harder. The harder I try, the less natural I am, the less jobs I book. It's a frustrating cycle.

Then I meet Adam, and this time the tables are turned. His heart is even more guarded than mine. He tries to keep me at arm's length, which makes me want him even more. It feels safe to be with a man who is so focused on his career that he won't make me the center of his universe. I fight for the relationship, which ends up lasting almost a decade. We are both driven by a burning desire to make our mark, and our dynamic is perfectly designed to catalyze our BEⵕOMING.

It's Adam who introduces me to psychedelics, thus awakening a part of me that has been offline since I began stifling my empathy at 10 years old.

SOUL CURRICULUM

We: The concept of a soul's curriculum is important, because without it, the premise that we are the co-creators of our reality—which we will dive into in the next chapter—doesn't hold water for very long.

If you've watched or read *The Secret* and found yourself intrigued by the Law of Attraction, you can't embark on the journey of manifestation without confronting the question: *If we really create our own reality through our thoughts and beliefs, how come so many human beings are born into a life of poverty and suffering? Did they willingly "create" that reality in the womb?*

We've sat long and hard with this question.

Why did Bee come into this life with learning disabilities so severe that his resulting lack of self-worth compelled him to overachieve to the point of burnout? And why did Azrya have to go through the trauma of "abandoning" her beloved grandmother, thus deeming herself unsafe to love and carrying that wound into all of her intimate relationships? We didn't consciously choose these things; they happened *to* us!

Or did they?

We've come to the conclusion that none of these circumstances make a whole lot of sense if we only consider them from the perspective of one lifetime. But if we zoom out and look at the trajectory of the soul's evolutionary journey over many lifetimes, it might make sense that—for the sake of experiencing the full spectrum of human sensation—a soul could choose to experience some form of challenge or suffering because there are invaluable and necessary lessons to be learned there.

This thesis would commonly be called reincarnation, which may activate the skeptic in you and possibly make you put this book down right now. If you do not resonate with that language and the concept of a soul having multiple lifetimes seems far-fetched if not completely implausible to you, don't despair. We aren't attached to reincarnation being True with a capital T, and we know firsthand that believing in multiple lifetimes is not something you can pick up in a book. It comes from cultivating a dialogue with your own soul. While we ourselves have had actual lived experiences of the "past life" phenomena or out-of-body experiences, many of which feel inexplicable and metaphysical in nature, we are also open to the possibility that our encounters with "the other side" could be explained through the more scientific lens of epigenetics instead.

Epigenetics is an emergent field in medicine that studies the way in which our DNA carries imprints (often traumatic ones) through our ancestral lineages and informs our present experience of reality—not just on the physical plane but also on the emotional and psycho-spiritual planes.

From this perspective, what some might call "past lives" could actually be zip files of experiential information stored in the genetic material of previous generations, and when a "memory" that feels real surfaces in our reality, despite the fact that it did not happen in this lifetime, it could be that a dormant part of our DNA came online and gave us access to an experience from one of our ancestors that they themself never transmuted.

Whether you choose to see it through the lens of reincarnation or epigenetics ultimately doesn't matter. Either frame will help you navigate challenges that seem beyond your control. Those challenges are likely the exact curriculum your soul signed up for to learn and mature from. The external circumstances of the culture, family, and environment you're born into as well as the internal circumstances of your disposition, proclivities, and "weaknesses" are the course material for your life and your soul's development.

On this note, it's important to distinguish the difference between being a victim of circumstance and getting stuck in victim consciousness, which is essentially when a victim creates such a strong identity around their trauma that it now defines them. This identity creates a narrative of victimhood which will keep looping until the trauma is faced, the emotions are fully felt, and the lessons (no matter how painful) are extracted from the traumatic experience. When that process completes itself, it is not uncommon for the traumatic event to transform into a desire to support others in healing from similar wounds. This transformation of perspective and energy means the trauma has been transmuted from shadow into light.

Reincarnation would see soul curriculum challenges as unresolved material from a previous lifetime, which a soul (mostly unconsciously) reactivates in this lifetime in order to give you the opportunity to complete the karmic pattern.

Epigenetics would see the challenges as coming from a genetic predisposition or a traumatic imprint within the inherited DNA, passed down through generations.

In both cases, the unique challenges we each face in our unique soul's curriculum actually contain invaluable gifts that allow us to mature into full embodiment and step into our life's purpose. The trick is to see these obstacles for the opportunities they are: to see them through the lens of love rather than the lens of fear.

Think of life like a school your soul is enrolled in. You are given the privilege of receiving a curriculum, and once you learn it and pass your exams, you are assigned a new, more advanced curriculum.

So there is no need to ever get frustrated or angry when life gives you more curriculum. It simply means that you have advanced and are ready for your next challenge. It is in the letting go of resistance to our soul's curriculum and accepting and embracing the opportunity that it is that we BƎϘOMƎ who we were always designed to be.

Can you feel the sweet humility in acknowledging that the universe has a plan for you that you can't necessarily understand yet? This lens challenges the deeply individualistic worldview that asserts "if I want something, I have to make it happen." It also challenges the concept of luck and randomness, which to us is actually quite relieving.

Truth is: *it's vulnerable when someone can see something that you can't see.*

There's a surrendering of control that has to occur in order for you to be receptive to that possibility, that reality: "Wow, life is bigger than me. I don't have to have it all figured out." Phew. What a beautiful moment of surrendering into the infinite dance with the great mystery! When you acknowledge, accept, and even celebrate that you're not meant to see the whole picture, you receive the gift of going on the cosmic scavenger hunt and—piece by piece—understanding the intelligent design of your life.

Now, this doesn't mean that the universe is going to handle everything for you. We're not talking about outsourcing your choices to some faraway God, which is why the term "co-creator" is key. Remember, you signed up for this! You are not separate from the intelligence that designed you. The masterpiece that is your life is yours to co-engineer, design, build, and manifest through the power of your free will, with the universe as your ally.

When you are in conscious dialogue with life in this way, participating actively with whatever circumstances have been given to you, you can start to engage with your assigned soul curriculum much more deliberately and speed up or slow down the process of learning. The universe will no longer need to throw you curveballs to get you to pay attention, like a teacher banging their fist on the table of a sleeping student. It will instead begin to dance with you as an equal partner in the game of life, constantly inviting you into deeper self-awareness, expansion, and Unfuckwithability. Instead of trying to resist or control your curriculum, you begin to eagerly anticipate the gifts contained within the next lesson.

The point isn't to graduate. The point is to learn to love the dance.

INVITATION #2:

Describe to the best of your ability :

- What do you think your soul's curriculum has been?

- What are the lessons you feel you have repeatedly been given the opportunity to learn?

- Are there any familiar patterns in the challenges you've faced?

- How committed are you to learning the lessons the universe assigned to you so that you can BEQOME the person you were designed to be?

- What tools or people currently available to you might help you move through your soul's curriculum?

3

TRADING TIMELINES

"Put your ass where your heart wants to be."

—Steven Pressfield

Bee: It's been eight months since my father got the diagnosis: stage 4 pancreatic cancer. I'll never forget the date. December 2, 2015. The moment I heard the news, I dropped everything I was doing, drove home, packed a bag, and moved in with my parents. Watching cancer eat away at my pops and best friend has been beyond heavy. Tonight is the first night in forever that I decide to take a load off and go out for margaritas to shoot the shit with a few old friends. I'm finally able to laugh for the first time in months. But the joy is short-lived; I come home around 10 p.m. to find my father face down on the counter in a puddle of spilled milk. He's out cold from all the meds. The kitchen is a mess. Delirious, he tried to make himself a latte before losing consciousness. Furious with myself for having stepped away, I fight back my tears, scoop up his limp body, and carry him to bed.

Two months later, we bury him.

For the next seven days after the funeral, I wake up at the crack of dawn, while my girlfriend Olga sleeps upstairs, and stare out over the Pacific Ocean from my desk. Death is a powerful teacher, and it has swept into my life and forced me to confront some hard truths about where I am following in my father's footsteps of letting fear drive my life. I sit and stare into the heavy silence as my gut churns, no longer able to ignore the two biggest places I am out of integrity in my life: my intimate partnership with Olga and my lack of purpose.

Olga and I have been together off and on for over three years, and the relationship has been filled with hot sex and slamming doors, sweet cuddles and hateful words used like weapons. My love for this woman is so real and so deep, it's hard to accept that the wounds we have opened and reopened within each other so many times have created scars that will never fade. Our melting pot of deep unprocessed insecurity, jealousy, rage, and abandonment trauma turn even the smallest disagreements into cataclysmic events. I have tried to end it many times, but never had the courage to truly cut the cords that connect us. My love for her intertwines with my fear of being alone, to the point where I cannot separate the two. Codependent, I keep finding myself back in her arms, even though in my heart of hearts I know neither of us are mature enough to repair what has been damaged and truly find lasting happiness with each other.

But now, something has shifted. Seeing my father shrivel up like a raisin as the cancer devoured his vital organs from the inside out has opened a window into my future, and now, sitting here utterly stripped awake, I am seeing the timelines of my life stretched out before me with sobering clarity.

As I reflect on all the things my father meant to me, I can't shake the memories of all our conversations about the what ifs. My father created extraordinary things in his lifetime, yet on his deathbed, he carried within him deep regret of having spent his whole life chasing future finish lines and not ever truly taking the time to enjoy the fruits of his labor. The energy of his regret is with me now as I make up my mind not to make the same mistakes.

On the seventh day, I hear Olga's feet on the stairs. She stops halfway down when she sees me staring out at the water. Without looking up at her, I simply say: "I don't want to do this anymore."

My voice carries with it a finality that I've never had before in this conversation with Olga, because it comes from the KNOWING I can't escape: that I must actually walk away for the last time. For the first time, I have the courage to finally claim that KNOWING and act on it.

My decision is cemented. I have chosen the timeline without her in it, because it will give me the time and space to B Ξ Q O M Ξ a man that can show up in his Truest Truth, which is the only way I can be an energetic match to a woman who can meet me in a healthy and devoted union. Who can meet me in hot sex, sweet cuddles, comforting words, and wide-open doors and who can find freedom in the depth of commitment.

Olga doesn't fight me on the separation this time. We're both exhausted. As I walk the house after she's removed all of her belongings, a Wayne Dyer quote becomes my mantra: "Life will give you the same exam over and over again until you pass it." The two exams I have been faced with over and over are staring me in the face again. One is in the romance department; the other is in the purpose department. I declare myself ready to pass both.

Stabilizing in this new timeline toward finding The One doesn't happen overnight. I am 44 years old now and seriously committed to finding this woman of my dreams, so—in my usual "if you want something, you've gotta make it happen" style—I turn dating into a career of sorts.

Yet the aching void within myself that had me entangled in a codependent and toxic dynamic in the first place is still gnawing at me when I venture back out into the dating pool, and I'm driven to fill it with an endless assortment of women. I couldn't remember all of their names if you paid me to. In the beginning, it takes me a few dates to discern whether there's potential with a woman, but soon I can tell in less than five minutes. That often doesn't stop me from sleeping with her, though. I have countless sexual encounters, but none of them can fill the void within me.

Then I run into Olga a few times over the summer. Sparks fly. We end up in bed together. I can feel the universe testing my resolve.

The passion, the comfort, the love that is still there between us is so tempting to return to...but I've been here before, and every time the whisper in my bones gets louder: *You know this won't work.*

I can't ignore the whisper anymore. The death of my father will not let me. I recommit to my new timeline.

Over the next three years, I reflect on my relationship with Olga and eventually begin to transcend the searing pain in my gut that activates every time I remember what it felt like to hold her in my arms. My heart starts to unclench as I begin to let go of the blame I've projected onto her. My nervous system slowly unwinds. The fire of fury in my belly fizzles, then subsides. I start taking radical ownership for my part in all of it and begin to realize that the way I was showing up never allowed her to feel safe enough to show up the way I needed her to. How could she be trusting when I was, in so many ways, hard as a rock?

My resentment turns to gratitude. I see the gifts wrapped in thorns and realize that everything we went through together was preparing me to be the kind of man that I've always wanted to be in a relationship: secure, communicative, open hearted, trusting. I keep deliberately anchoring into the timeline in which I am building a life with my soul mate. The choices that are not in alignment with that timeline, such as sleeping with women who I know aren't The One, begin to make it harder and harder to look myself in the eye until eventually it just becomes glaringly obvious: All the searching and seeking is the exact *opposite* energy of what I'm calling in. It's time to stop all of the external action and become still.

Fuck.

Being still makes the incessant Doer in me squirm, but a quiet voice within urges me to trust in the Non-Doing.

With the amount of energy and focus it takes to bring a freight train hurtling down the tracks to a full stop, I gradually quit dating and decide to let Her come to me.

It's not easy. The lonely nights wear on me. Sometimes I cave, send a text I know I shouldn't send, then find myself teetering on the edge of falling off my new timeline again. But I keep catching myself, course correcting and stabilizing. A therapist once told me that I wouldn't find my soul mate until I was living my purpose. I'm making progress in the romance department, but when it comes to my purpose, I'm still way off track, as becomes abundantly clear when a business partner calls me one day with devastating news.

A New OS

I hang up the phone, my heart rate sending hot currents of blood coursing through my throbbing temples. *What the fuck just happened?* I think I just got hit in the face with a sledgehammer.

In a daze, I make my way to the hallway mirror. Facing my reflection, I replay the events leading up to this moment: My friend presenting me with the most lucrative business opportunity I've seen in my entire career. My decision to go all in and invest millions. I'm as shrewd as they come. But this deal just went sideways in a major way, and salvaging it is impossible without a lawsuit that will cost me millions more and years of my life. Even then, there's no guarantee I'll recover the money I invested. I feel sick to my stomach.

Why? Because I'm a greedy asshole and was seduced by the legit $100MM exit valuation I was forecasting would happen in the first two to three years of the investment. *Dad dying wasn't enough for you to stop chasing the shiny objects, huh?* The cruel voice in my head taunts me. *What a hypocrite you are, telling everyone you are done with making more money, saying you want to live a life of purpose, of impact. Bullshit. All you know how to do is chase the dollar. You'll never do more than write a few checks a year to charity.* The voice is mean, but it's not wrong. I fucked up.

This time, chasing the dollar may have just cost me and my kids everything. Lying in bed in the fetal position, I ask myself how I could have gotten so far off track. I knew more money wasn't going to fulfill me, and yet the moment the universe tested my resolve, I slipped right back into the old pattern. *Holy shit*, I realize, staring at the wall like a corpse. *I don't trust myself at all. Something needs to change.*

Endless calls with lawyers ensue. I am distraught; I feel violated. Sitting at my desk one day, calculating every last worst-case scenario possible in my financial forecasting spreadsheet, I suddenly remember the stack of papers I've collected from various personal development retreats and leadership organizations I've attended over the years.

I open the drawer and pull out a folder, 10 inches thick. Leafing through the vast array of exercises, articles, and transformational tools, a spark of inspiration illuminates the doom and gloom of my internal state just long enough for me to realize:

If I can't trust myself to make healthy decisions, that must mean two things:

1. *I don't know myself well enough to be able to trust myself.*
2. *I need to design a trustworthy system that can help me avoid taking risks with unacceptable consequences.*

The project starts out as a hobby, but quickly becomes all consuming. In the following months I spend about 500 hours designing what I start calling my Personal Operating System. I justify the time invested by telling myself that this will be a valuable tool to pass onto my kids. I go beyond granular. I need to know *why* I am the way I am. With a fine-tooth comb, I analyze my entire past, from birth onward. I shine a light into every crevice of my life, contemplating my relationship to my family, women, career, money, health, success, failure, legacy, and my intentions for the future. I vow that the next time the universe tests me, I will not fail the purpose exam again.

The 200-page Personal Operating System becomes my bible. I carry a hard copy of it everywhere I go, scribbling memos all over it, updating it again and again and printing a new version each quarter. I have been a member of various leadership organizations, such as YPO (Young Presidents Organization), Vistage, Tiger-21, and Alder, and I have a solid network of impressive CEOs. I share my newfound tool with my forum brothers and sisters, and some of them really resonate with it and incorporate it as a guiding resource in their life. I see that we're all spending countless hours on our business plans, but our personal lives are falling to the wayside. I start to flirt with the idea that sharing this process I just walked myself through with my peers could become part of my purpose. I never saw myself as a coach and am not ready to claim that title, but this template has become a lifeline and I feel like it's needed in my community.

Meanwhile, the legal battle drags on. The case is so complex and messy, months go by with very little progress. At the same time that I decide to quit dating anyone who doesn't have the potential to be my soulmate, I also decide I'm going to stop investing and instead focus on finally being of service.

The first step on this path of purpose is to educate myself. I decide that I'll read all the books and attend more workshops and retreats. Then, maybe in a couple of years, I'll be ready to share my Operating System Template and my blessings with the world. *Yeah, that feels safe,* my ego thinks. *Let's hang out in the comfort zone until it's not so risky, then take the leap.*

Turns out, the universe seldom lets it be that easy.

Instead, Azrya walks into my life and swiftly catapults me onto the most accelerated timeline of B ☰ Q O M I N G—*everything I didn't know I wanted.*

Timelines

We: We'll use this term "timelines" frequently throughout the book to describe the various versions of reality that are available to us at any given moment through the power of choice, but first: a one-paragraph crash course on quantum physics.

The quantum field is the infinite energetic field we are all a part of, which is made up of frequencies that carry information. That information exists in the quantum as un-manifest potential, meaning it has not yet been collapsed into form. We navigate our normal day-to-day reality—which we like to call the 3D, aka the third dimension of time and space—with our five senses and are constantly making thousands of micro-decisions that solidify our experience of reality into one particular timeline. Most of those decisions are happening through our autonomic nervous system, which is the subconscious part of us that enables our organs to perform their duties without requiring instructions and allows us to drive a car or tie our shoelaces without much conscious thought.

But in the same way that we can get really comfortable taking the same route to work every day, other subconscious programs get deeply ingrained in us as well, and many of those stand in direct opposition to our soul's expansion. In order to make a "quantum leap" into a brand-new version of ourselves and truly embody our greatest potential, we must learn to temporarily transcend the third dimension of time and space and tap into the field of infinite potential where all timelines exist simultaneously. It's hard to understand this with the logical mind because we have been so conditioned to think about reality in a fixed and linear way, so don't be alarmed if this sounds like a bunch of gibberish to you.

In Bee's example, we see how his intention to call in his soulmate required him to trade in the timeline he was on with Olga and make the difficult choice of letting a woman he deeply loved go. Once he did, he was one step closer to calibrating his energetic signature to align with The One, but his pattern of constant dating was coming from a place of lack, and therefore it wasn't a vibrational match to the caliber of woman he was calling in.

Similarly, the trust-breach moment from his childhood that had been such a huge component of his soul curriculum manifested itself as the lawsuit, which catapulted him onto the timeline of creating the Personal Operating System as a tool to guide his life and has since become a foundational component of our B Ξ Q O M I N G course materials.

When Benjamin invested in the business deal that went sideways, what he *thought* he wanted was to get a 20x return on his investment. What he *really* wanted was to be forced out of his comfort zone of chasing the dollar and, instead, wake up and finally step into his true calling. Can you see how the very wound of deep distrust that began in Little League directly informed the activation of Bee's most fulfilling life purpose? This is a perfect example of what we mean when we say that our traumas contain our greatest gifts, if only we are willing to finally meet them fully.

Another example of quantum timelines at play is this: Imagine you've made a commitment to your health, which includes eliminating alcohol and working out at 6 a.m. every morning. The first few days are a breeze. Then, the weekend comes and you are hanging out with a bunch of your closest friends at a restaurant. After dinner, they all spontaneously decide to go out to a bar for drinks and music. You are faced with a choice: abandon your commitment and submit to the tug of the herd or remain steadfast in what you said you would do. You are now "between" timelines. The default is often to say "fuck it, I'll get on track again tomorrow," have a drink, dance till 2 a.m. and skip your morning workout. The problem is, when you play that timeline out, it tends to lead to a whole slew of future "fuck it" moments, which—over time—don't deliver the health results you are seeking. Going against the herd, on the other hand, requires more energy in the now, but in the long run, it leads to building trust within yourself to follow through with your commitment and puts you on the fastest timeline to being healthy and fit.

We're not saying it's never the right choice to have a Mezcal margarita and get groovy, but we are suggesting that the benefit of any choice you make really boils down to your ability to discern when it's really worth saying "fuck it" and when that "fuck it" is just coming from a familiar, self-limiting habit. Discernment is key, and discernment is usually only possible when there's internal spaciousness to tune in and listen to the voice of the Truest Truth that communicates beyond programmed, default responses. In this particular scenario, stepping outside of the restaurant and taking a few deep, intentional breaths with your eyes closed can provide the clarity to commit to the timeline that will serve you best. **The more you take the time and space to tune in to the voice of your Truest Truth, the more you develop the ability to discern between what you want *most* and what you want *now*.**

What may seem like a menial choice point in the moment, when extrapolated over time, leads to two distinctly different versions of the future you. Just like if you have two cruise ships going in the same direction, but with two degrees difference in course, over time they'd end up on two entirely different spots on the globe.

The amount of choices we are confronted with on a daily basis are astounding and require a tremendous amount of our vital life-force energy. Smaller ones include whether to get the almond milk latte with sugar or without or whether to be the first one to say sorry after an argument. Bigger ones are whether to stay in a relationship or start over with someone new. Whether to take a job that pays the bills, hedge a risky bet that promises a fortune, or follow your passion even if it scares you shitless.

We've discovered a simple tool that will help you cut through all the noise and make the call that is truly in alignment with your Truest Truth—and it's called the Full Fuck Yes.

The Full Fuck Yes

"I use my Full Fuck Yes to discern what I want **most** over what I want **now**."

If there are infinite timelines to choose from in every moment, how do you know which one is the right one for you?

We choose to believe that there's a golden thread that weaves through all the possibilities, which we call your Full Fuck Yes (FFY) timeline. It's like hitting the vein of gold amidst layers of rock.

There's an unmistakable sparkle that erupts inside of your emotional body when you tap into the FFY timeline, for it contains within its frequency all the instructions required to activate the full embodiment of the highest version of yourself.

Getting to that voice, the one that resonates at the frequency of your Truest Truth, requires spending time in reflection and meditative stillness in order to develop the discernment required to truly live in alignment with your Truest Truth. Over time, through the art of witnessing your thoughts rather than identifying with them and deepening the connection to your breath rather than being lost in the chatter of the monkey mind, that inner voice of wisdom begins to communicate more and more clearly.

All of your soul's curriculum is designed to get you closer and closer to matching the vibration of your Full Fuck Yes timeline, so while we firmly believe in the power of free will to choose your own experience, the paradox exists in the fact that your Full Fuck Yes timeline is already written. How, when, and with what degree of ease and grace you calibrate to it is entirely up to you to decide, in every moment anew.

It's not uncommon for the Full Fuck Yes timeline to scare you as much as it intrigues you. Why? Because it often comes at a cost, and that cost is the comfort zone of your known reality. Once you make contact with your Truest Truth, it's hard to unsee what it has to show you, for what it has to show you often requires facing some difficult truths that come with tough decisions. Maybe it feels selfish or even irresponsible to really step onto your Full Fuck Yes timeline. Maybe you have concerns that your spouse, your friends, your boss will not get it; maybe you even fear losing them entirely.

We want to invite you to trust in the benevolence of the FFY. In our experience, it's never going to create a situation where one person has to lose so the other can gain. If it's truly the Full Fuck Yes timeline and it's free from fear-based distortions, then it will not generate win-lose situations, only present win-win circumstances for everyone involved.

That doesn't mean everyone will choose to see it that way. But it does mean that the opportunity is there. Whether those closest to you choose to meet you there is up to them, and their readiness to commit to their process of B Ξ Q O M I N G. That is their soul's curriculum to navigate, and you cannot do that work for them.

Truly stepping onto the FFY timeline might initially create conflict—especially in your intimate partnership or family dynamics. But that conflict can be a catalyst for the deepest union and connection you have ever experienced. It can be the fertile soil from which more intimate, authentic, and meaningful relationships are born, even if it is not initially evident how.

What's required is the willingness to face the fear that is keeping you *the same.*

Welcome to your chosen destiny.

INVITATION #3:

- Look into the past. Make a list of the pivotal moments in your life when you were given multiple timelines to choose from. What were they? Did your choices bring you closer or further away from your Full Fuck Yes? Are there any patterns worth noting here?

- Look into the future: What timelines do you currently have in front of you? Which timeline will most honor the person you are **BEQOMING**?

- How close do you currently feel you are to living your Full Fuck Yes timeline?

- What resources might help you step into your Full Fuck Yes timeline?

4

IF LOVE IS THE ANSWER,
FEAR IS THE TEACHER

"The hardest thing of all is to find a black cat
in a dark room, especially if there is no cat."

—Confucius

Azrya: It's February 28, 2015. I am sitting in the sprawling living room of a massive mansion perched on the edge of an ocean-side cliff, taking in the majestic orchids and white goddess statues that adorn the candle-lit space. All around me, people are setting up yoga mats and pillows, forming rows of semicircles around where the shaman will sit, up against floor-to-ceiling windows. Communication is happening in hushed tones, and plastic buckets are being handed out. It's hard to imagine that this church-like space will soon be filled with the sound of intense vomiting, which in these circles is referred to as "the purge" and allows for the healing and purification of mind, body, and spirit.

From what I've gathered, there are two kinds of people in the world. Those who have drank Ayahuasca, and those who haven't.

This will be my first time ingesting the psychoactive Amazonian brew, and I am finally ready to meet this ancient "Grandmother" entity that is said to have a distinct feminine quality to it and has been served in ceremonial contexts by Indigenous South American shamans for generations.

A year ago, I watched my partner and ally Adam go through the most profound awakening with Ayahuasca and viscerally felt his transformation catalyze my own. Everyone I've spoken to about this plant medicine has vastly different experiences and perspectives, but the one thing everyone seems to agree on is this: *intention is everything.* The experience will be shaped by my *why*, my reason for being here. From what I've heard, Grandmother has the capacity to blast you into the multiverse, *and* she has the capacity to land you headfirst in the sacred shit. Ayahuasca commands respect and reverence, precisely because the egoic mind doesn't have a fighting chance once the medicine floods your system with DMT—dimethyltryptamine—also known as the "God" molecule.

I'm not here for spiritual tourism or to get high, so I've carefully and sincerely meditated on my intention leading up to this night. At this point in my spiritual journey, I've read the standard "Law of Attraction" literature, I've had some real epiphanies during meditation, and I've laid on the dusty playa at Burning Man, tasting a technicolor type of liberation I never knew was possible. But while all of those experiences sincerely tapped me into the pulse of the profound, something in my day-to-day life is still missing.

This is why I'm here tonight. I want to know whether the aching awareness that I am supposed to *be* more, *know* more, and *give* more is real or whether it's an illusion. I am 28 years old, and the Hollywood career I once so aspired to pour myself into feels increasingly vapid and empty.

It's like I'm staring right at an answer that is somehow obscured by an invisible veil. I have to know what's on the other side.

My intention tonight is, *"Dear Grandmother. Please show me what I'm missing."*

Finally, close to midnight, it's time. The low-toned chatter in the room abruptly subsides as the Brazilian shaman enters the space wearing a massive headdress and traditional ceremonial garb. The energy becomes focused. Fifty-five people all attempt to mentally prepare for the unpreparable by sitting upright and sharpening their inhales. One by one, we kneel in front of the shaman, who peers at us through ancient eyes, then pours a small cup of the dark viscous brew for us to drink in humble silence.

The pungent taste is reminiscent of fermented molasses and sends shudders down my spine. I return to my mat and take my position. *I'm going to sit up all night*, I tell myself. *Cute, kid.* The moment the medicine hits, I am in the fetal position with my sleeping bag over my head. *Holy fuck.* My body legitimately feels like it's rapidly shrinking in size, until I am a fetus inside of a womb. Translucent walls of a glowing uterus surround me as I float, suspended in embryonic fluid, my nervous system flooded with the sensation of being utterly held and at home.

Back to the source we go.

The visions that ensue are so beyond high-def, it feels like I'm inside of a holographic IMAX movie. I am now in direct contact with an intelligence that is so vast, so ancient, so loving yet so fierce that I have no choice but to sit up and bow my head in reverence. Grandmother has the steering wheel of my consciousness now, and all I can do is surrender to her.

As the journey intensifies, fear floods my body. I start to resist the visions. The moment I do, they turn on me, taking on grotesque forms. *Surrender,* something inside me whispers. *Lean in instead of shying away.* The moment I follow the instructions, the fear disappears and the visions become beautiful again. I have just been given the most important tool with which to navigate my entire human experience: non-resistance to What Is, and a felt KNOWING that all fear is an illusion.

So you think you're missing something?

The medicine communicates not in words but in KNOWING.

Here's what you came to see.

In a flash, Aya shows me snippets of all the auditions I attended over the course of my flailing acting career and all the disappointment I felt when I didn't land the gig time and time again. *Booking those jobs would have all been distractions from finding your real purpose,* she reveals. *You were designed for something much bigger than* CSI: New York. *It's time for you to let go of what you thought you wanted and make space for everything you didn't know you wanted.*

My energy body starts to expand until I feel eight feet tall, beaming light from every pore in all directions. I have never felt more powerful. *This power is the power of infinite love*, the medicine tells me. *This is your natural state, beyond fear, beyond distortion. Now watch.*

I see a highlight reel of my future self, coaching A-list celebrities and high-net worth CEOs, activating them at a DNA level. I watch how the impact that is created in them, their families, businesses, and brands ripples out into the world and catalyzes global transformation and planet-wide healing. *Your eight years in the entertainment industry have not been in vain,* Aya goes on to assure me. *Turning media into medicine at scale is a crucial part of your code. Through sharing the stories of your life, you will awaken millions and initiate them into* B≡QOMING.

I see the machine that is Hollywood going through a death, re-birth process as the true responsibility of media and storytelling and its impact on programming the hearts and minds of humanity becomes obvious. *The most powerful people on the planet are awakening, and you will be one of their guides*, the medicine declares. *You will show them how to channel the power of their love into designing a new world.*

But wait a minute, my inner voice pleads, *I don't know a single celebrity or CEO. I've never coached a single person. How am I supposed to execute this massive assignment?*

Grandmother chuckles. *You will be supported. We are in this together. Welcome home.*

Then the visions disappear, and I'm back in the living room, surrounded by 55 grunting, sighing, and vomiting strangers.

Holy shit. In a couple of hours, my entire identity construct was shattered, rearranged, and reconstructed. I realize with an incredible lightness that I will never be the same.

Feeling suddenly very sober, I decide I must celebrate this pivotal realization by going outside. The ceremony is still in full swing; everyone is in a process, amplified by the chanting shamans. I search for the back door of the house, find it, and sneak out, my face instantly lighting up as I am greeted by the spectacular night sky and a chorus of chirping frogs. Joy floods my body, and I find my feet magnetically drawn to an epic view where the ocean is illuminated by a dazzling moon, framed by a dramatic display of silver-tipped clouds. It's so gorgeous, every molecule of my being squeals in delight. Cold, strong wind tugs at my long dark hair and clothes, but thankfully I'm prepared and am wearing multiple layers, including boots and a bathrobe over my heavy sweater. Mesmerized by the luminescent sky, I skip down a few terraced steps, feeling adventurous and marveling at how present I am with the exquisite beauty that surrounds me, when—*BAM.*

Freezing cold water engulfs me, filling my nose and mouth as I sink down, solid ground having just vanished under my feet. My limbs kick and struggle, fighting gravity. I swim upward and yank myself out of the infinity pool I just obliviously walked into. The medicine is still with me as I collapse in a puddle on the cement, soaked to the bone. *There's **being** in the moment, and then there's being **lost** in the moment,* Aya says sternly, but with a twinkle in her non-physical eye. I chuckle to myself. *Got it, Grandma.*

Later I find out, had I ventured 30 feet in either direction of the pool, I would have walked right off the edge of the cliff. But that doesn't deter me from celebrating the new timeline I was just catapulted on.

Glowing, I leave the ceremony the next day, radiating invincibility. *Bring it, universe. Let's awaken humanity; I'm fucking ready.*

Then, reality hits me like a ton of bricks. Turns out, I am not an eight-foot-tall superhero beaming cosmic love from every pore. I'm actually still just an unemployed actress living in a one-bedroom apartment in Santa Monica who is trying to figure out if *The Secret* is full of shit or not. Global impact *what? How?!* I need a nap.

With no support other than Adam, who is as deeply committed to his awakening as I am to mine, I begin the arduous journey of trying to integrate my experience. I quickly learn that tasting the vastness of our power can initially feel more traumatizing than staying in the comfort zone of our limitations, for it creates a painful gap between what's *possible* and what is *now* that demands to be closed.

I can't unknow what the medicine allowed me to feel so unequivo-cally, so pretending like my divine assignment was just some trippy hallucination isn't an option.

I have to become this person that I tasted a glimpse of in my vision.

I will do whatever it takes.

The first tangible step I know I must take is to quit my day job. *Oh God. How the hell am I supposed to survive without this cushy steady paycheck I've depended on for over six years?!* Working for the German version of *E! News*, translating celebrity gossip, and doing the voi-ceovers for the likes of Kim Kardashian, Paris Hilton, and Miley Cyrus felt like a dream gig when I first got hired, but now all I can see is how I am *literally* contributing my voice to feeding the col-lective Ego, which is the opposite of what the medicine has shown me I'm here to do.

My heart urges me to leap, but my mind is pumping the brakes. *Oh hell no, you're not quitting without a backup plan! Be rational. Get a few coaching clients and some steady income, then quit.*

Sounds so logical, right? Except I've just been blasted into a realm far beyond logic. I'm awakening to the reality of vibration, and the energy of hesitation I'm projecting into the universe is directly blocking me from landing in certainty.

Over the next six months, it becomes glaringly obvious that try-ing to leap while desperately clinging to my comfort zone is going to get me nowhere. Staring at "I AM ABUNDANT" sticky-note affirmations on my bathroom mirror isn't going to cut it. There are subconscious fears blocking me that I won't be able to see until I poke them right in the eyeball. It's time to get radical.

I end up quitting my job with $2,000 to my name. It's free-fall time.

Survival fears propel me into action. I find solace in deciding I'm going to "make it happen no matter what." I replace going to the park, meditating, and being in my divine feminine flow with end-less hours hunched at my laptop trying to build click-funnels. I am exhausted and stressed out *just like every brand-new aspiring sole proprietor should be, right???* Fuck. NO. This isn't it.

Just as I'm teetering on the verge of despair, a life coach named Andrea pops into my reality and encourages me to ditch the strat-egy, go beyond the limitations of the mind, tap into the quantum field, channel the information I need in the moment, and attract the clients I want to serve by mastering my vibration. "It doesn't have to be hard at all, unless you decide it should be," she says to me, with a stress-free giggle.

Something inside me KNOWS this woman is onto something.

I decide I need her to help me plug back into what I already know and give me permission to finally fully trust it. My heart races as I call to tell her I want to work with her. I'm already cringing before I hear the price. Sure enough, her coaching package costs $8,000. *Yikes.* I have $2,000 to my name. My rent is due in two weeks. My cortisol spikes as hot and cold flashes send *code red* signals to my brain. *This is crazy; run for the hills!* But my heart knows it's time to go all in.

"All I have is two grand. If I give it all to you, can we get started?" I incredulously hear myself asking her.

"Of course," she says. "Does PayPal work?"

Once I clean out my account, I actually feel oddly relieved. Seeing zero was my worst fear, and now it's here, and so all that's left to do is just surrender into the void.

Within three weeks of sending Andrea that first payment, I effortlessly manifest $18,000 through signing two coaching clients and landing an acting gig. I realize: it was the willingness to face the fear, go all in, and then completely surrender my attachment to outcome that allowed for that to happen. I am sure I cracked the manifestation code.

I'll never have money problems again! I declare. Boy, am I wrong. Scarcity consciousness runs deep, as it turns out, and I end up cycling through zero several more times over the next couple of years, each time forcing me to stabilize in greater and greater trust.

From that moment forward, fear becomes my greatest teacher for embodying more love and abandoning my comfort zone becomes a full-time job. Each time I take the leap, it brings me one step closer to landing on my new timeline, but the cost is high. Everything that is familiar is steadily stripped away. Eventually, I fire my acting agents and managers, give up my apartment and my community, relinquish most of my belongings, transparently share my process on social media, and start traveling on one-way tickets across the world in search of my tribe.

My journey takes me to Mexico, Costa Rica, Bali, Australia, and Africa. I continue to study with Ayahuasca as my main plant medicine teacher, and she helps chisel me into the person who can actually have global impact. Part of that chiseling requires the constant relinquishing of who I thought I was supposed to be.

A Complete Reset

One day, about three years after that first ceremony, a woman with healing gifts confronts me with a KNOWING I've held my entire life but never had the courage to admit.

"I hope you won't be offended," she says, "but Melinda is not your name. There's a new name wanting to come through."

The moment she says it, I know she's right, and the name Azrya crystalizes as a tool with which to claim the woman I know I am destined to B Ξ Q O M Ξ.

Committing to Azrya makes my hands shake as I confront all the eye-rolling judgment I've held toward people who changed their name. *Will people think I'm just another white chick who drank too much Ayahuasca and has deluded herself into believing she's found her purpose by flaunting her savior complex on Instagram?* The answer is *Yes, some will think exactly that.* It doesn't matter. I know this decision will solidify the rebirth I've been midwifing myself through.

But changing my name is not enough. Every rebirth requires a death to precede it. The claiming demands a complete reset. It requires an initiation. So I ask Adam, my steady companion on this road of transformation, to shave my head on Facebook Live, letting the last tendrils of my false identity fall away and allowing myself to be seen, truly seen, beyond any conditioned ideas of what it means to be beautiful. Hundreds message me, thanking me for sharing my process and celebrating me in my chosen transformation.

I continue teaching others what I'm learning on the spiritual path. My clients are not CEOs or celebrities; they are people like me who are seeking to understand how to feel at home in a world that feels like it was never designed for them to thrive. As I deepen my practice, face my darkest fears, cry, scream, purge, and celebrate my way to liberation, I continue to make choices that stabilize me in the new timeline. The version of me that I tasted in that first ceremony begins to come more and more into focus. Every leap of faith brings me one step closer to merging with her fully.

On my journey, I begin to find members of my soul family and unite them into a tribe. One by one they reveal themselves. Liana, Elana, Anáil, Zahara, Blu, Briana, Anthony, Bear Heart, Matthew, and Adrian form the inner core, and there are many more incredible souls that I feel an instant spark of familiarity with. What connects us is our almost irrational trust in something much greater than meets the eye. We've all been shown similar visions and blueprints for a new humanity, and we are all equally committed to contributing our unique notes to the symphony of life. As we bond and our timelines merge, they strengthen. We all begin to stabilize more and more in the shared vision, sharing gazes across crowded rooms that say, *No, you're not crazy. The more beautiful world we've caught glimpses of is not just a faraway dream. It's an ever-blossoming reality. I see it too.*

Slowly but surely, I begin to penetrate circles of power, wealth, and influence and quickly learn that I cannot be a guide for just anybody's B Ξ Q O M I N G, that there must be a unique soul contract between us that cannot be described, only felt. I don't know what I'm looking for exactly, but I'm definitely looking for something. A click. A moment of recognition. The Full Fuck Yes.

In order to magnetize and meet those soul connections, I must let go of the one thing that has stayed consistent, safe, and steady for the last 10 years: my relationship with Adam. The medicine confirms that our time to part ways has come. We both KNOW that we have been stripped awake in the container of this union, taken turns catalyzing profound growth within each other, and now, we are both feeling the itch to spread our wings and fly solo. With heart-wrenching gratitude for the extraordinary journey we shared, we set each other free and consciously uncouple.

In full surrender mode, I allow my intuition to guide me back to LA, where I become the steward of a property that I call The Mothership. I curate a small team of soul allies and start implementing my vision of running retreats and filming a documentary.

But there's a puzzle piece still missing, and I realize that puzzle piece must be an investor *who gets it*. Who is awake enough to see beyond ROI and is ready to go all in on helping me execute this vision of global impact. I am ready to raise millions on behalf of my cause, and I KNOW that whoever is going to invest in me doesn't need a business plan. Their own, inexplicable KNOWING will be their compass.

I travel all around the world. Supported by my cosmic brother Adrian, a coaching client turned ally who greenlights my first documentary project, I attend the Blockchain Convergence in Tokyo, visit a huge hemp conference in Denver, drink Ayahuasca in the Colombian jungle with a multi-generational tribe of Indigenous shamans, attend the Sundance Film Festival in Park City, and find myself in a remote cabin in Norway getting tattooed by a Hungarian savant—all within six months. Every time I arrive in a new location, in front of a rolling camera, I set a powerful intention to steward $11MM within the next year. The claiming of that number scares the shit out of me. I have literally no idea how that is going to happen, let alone how I will manage my overhead at The Mothership the following month. But I choose to trust the *why* that lives underneath the number, and that *why* is coming from a deep KNOWING that all of the visions about supporting others in their B Ξ Q O M I N G at scale are ready to actualize. In fact, I trust so deeply that I stop charging set price points for my coaching packages and instead begin experimenting with what I call the Free Will Investment model, which means that the client can choose to pay me whatever amount they deem appropriate after the work is completed, or not. Most months, it works out beautifully and all expenses are covered. But then I get so busy working on digital Media as Medicine content that I don't organically connect with anyone who I am excited to facilitate for.

UPLEVELING

With three days left before my $12,000 rent is due, it's now getting down to the wire. Trying to take any linear action, such as calling in a last-minute client, won't work in time, plus it just doesn't feel like that approach is coming from a place of inspired Full Fuck Yes energy. So I do what I have been practicing for five years. I hold the intention (the *why*) with clarity and conviction and surrender all attachment to outcome, observing how calm I feel and reflecting on the fact that the same situation a year ago would have had me sweating bullets.

That evening, my friend Anthony swings by for a tea and a chat. "Hey, I'm heading to a sound bath if you want to join," he says. *You should stay home and figure out how the fuck you're going to pay your rent, woman!* My fear-based ego insists. But when I tune into the truer voice beneath the logic, I feel a pull to go. "I'm in," I say spontaneously, grabbing my coat.

After the sound bath ends, a beautiful and elegant blonde woman in her mid-40s who I've never seen before walks over, introduces herself to me as Rachel, and then looks right into my soul with her baby blue eyes. "This is going to sound very strange, but I recognize you from my dream last night," she says. *Interesting.* We chat for a few moments about our shared passion for plant medicine work and exchange information.

The following day, we speak on the phone, and I invite her to come by The Mothership after she completes an Ayahuasca ceremony that she happens to be attending that weekend. When she arrives, we walk the property and I share my vision for the land with her. Even though we are essentially strangers, she somehow understands my *why* exactly and clearly sees how this land can serve as a safe haven for transformation in the chaotic landscape of LA. "So how can you be supported right now?" she asks sincerely, before heading out.

I share honestly with her that the only thing missing is the funding to keep things going. A couple hours after she leaves, my phone pings. It's a text from Rachel.

Rachel: On my drive home I realized the act of working with or investing in this beautiful land and its mission would be an external admission of who I am to myself and others. I think my deep fear of acting from my true, authentic self was brightly illuminated in our conversation today. To heal this block, I am ready to commit $25,000 into this cosmic venture right now. As a gift.

My eyes fill with tears as I read her words. *Wow. The trust paid off again. Literally.*

Within 48 hours, the money is wired into my account as an act of unconditional love from a perfect stranger.

Once again, the universe delivered pure magic in the most unexpected ways, all because I finally learned to accept what the medicine has been telling me from the very beginning: that I am unconditionally provided for as long as I am living and breathing my *why*.

It's been five years since my first ceremony with Ayahuasca, and I have relentlessly thrown myself headfirst into B Ξ Q O M I N G who I need to be in order to execute my mission. It's time to let go and receive.

I begin to relax. I begin to come home to my body. After 10 years of monogamy with Adam, followed by 10 months of celibacy, I begin to consider dating again.

That's when Benjamin Bequer walks into my life and changes the game. In his wake, my trusted teacher Fear is at the ready, armed with a whole new batch of lessons in surrender.

BEYOND FEAR

We: We believe that, at their core, all feelings boil down to love or fear, and that both are powerful forces of nature. In our eyes, fear is merely the absence of love, but the absence of love is not to be underestimated. At the source level—the dimension of infinite oneness—it's all love; death is no less sacred or valuable an experience than life is. But in this physical dimension of time and space, danger and death are expressions of polarity. They manifest themselves as "real"—meaning while the soul is immortal, the human body is not. In fact, it has thousands of years of stored evidence in its genetic code that life on planet Earth is painful, scary, and— eventually—always deadly.

As Will Smith said: "Danger is very real, but fear is a choice." Most would agree that fear has a time and place. That it's an alarm system built into our biology, which has allowed us to survive unimaginable hardships throughout our brutal human history and still serves us today.

But does it *really*?

Is it possible to evolve beyond fear, just like we evolved beyond needing hair all over our bodies? Could we leave fear behind like a technology that has gone obsolete?

We're not sure anyone can answer that question just yet, but we've certainly noticed our relationship to fear has dramatically changed as its power over us has diminished through the full embracing of it as a valued teacher. We love Robert Heller's notion that *"fear is just excitement without breath."*

No matter who you are, you will inevitably be confronted with "dangers" barreling toward you in the form of financial stresses, relationship conflicts, daily anxieties, etc. Just like Azrya powerfully experienced in her first ceremony, every moment provides us with a choice point. Do we run and hide from these things, or do we stand and breathe them into the deepest caverns of our heart, thus alchemizing them through the power of our conscious choice?

Fear steers the ship, until we actively decide that we're ready for Love to take over. Kind of like switching from Windows to Mac, there's a learning curve. It's a completely different operating system.

Learning to face fear helps us use it as a portal to greater love. We cannot bypass fear; it is an intrinsic and important part of being human. Fear is a teacher because it shows us precisely where we lack love within ourselves. Like a homing device, we can follow the feeling of fear—which is usually experienced as contraction, closing, or withholding—to the parts of ourselves that are most starved for love. When love returns, it is usually experienced as expansion, warmth, and well-being.

Sometimes the feeling of fear isn't as strong or obvious and expresses itself as something more manageable, albeit pervasive, such as resistance or judgment. In *The War of Art*, Steven Pressfield talks extensively about this internal resistance, and how it is intent on sabotaging your creator consciousness at all costs. He gives profound advice on overcoming this resistance, but his relationship to resistance is also fairly antagonistic, which allows for traction but ultimately keeps us locked in a state of conflict with ourselves. We believe that resistance can be overcome, not by going to war with it but rather by understanding why it's here and loving it into submission.

Judgment is always a sign that fear lurks beneath the surface, for it is a protection mechanism, a way to create a safe distance, even if just through the subtle workings of an inner narrative of division. Judging someone's appearance, for example, is usually a quick way to find one's own insecurities about how we look. We are constantly projecting judgment and shame on others in order to distract ourselves from our own deepest wounds.

As Matt Kahn said, "Judgment is released by loving the one who judges."

As Azrya says, "We cannot heal that which we are busy judging."

Embrace judgment and fear as the teachers they are. If you follow their invitation to look deeper within, they will allow you to discover secret gems amidst the soil of your subconscious. The vehicle with which to navigate yourself through to these teachers is the ability to marry your awareness with your breath. This doesn't require fancy breathwork techniques. All it requires is the willingness to close your eyes, bring all of your focus to your inhales and your exhales, and let everything else fall away. Do that for 10 minutes every time you feel stressed, anxious, or afraid and watch your relationship to these energies transform.

The Dreaded Fear Pocket

Imagine yourself on a plane. You're gliding along through the clouds, sipping your mimosa and watching *Mrs. Doubtfire* on the classics channel when suddenly—you hit a pocket of air and the whole plane shakes, shudders, jerks, and dips. What happened? You encountered turbulence. So what do you do? Do you freak out? Argue vehemently with the flight attendant that this shouldn't be happening? Make it mean the plane is going down?

Or do you just surrender into the sensation and ride it out, trusting that "this too shall pass"?

The same is true for our emotional landscape. Sometimes we're coasting along, and then suddenly, we hit a fear pocket that manifests itself as internal turbulence. The heart clenches, the throat closes, the gut ties itself in knots.

This is actually normal. We're human and we feel things. The problem is, most of the time when we encounter fear (or any "negative" emotion on the shadow side of the spectrum), we tend to freak out, argue that this shouldn't be happening, and make it mean that everything is screwed. If our EQ, our emotional intelligence, has not been cultivated, we *identify* with the sensations instead of simply *witnessing* them as they pass through.

Fear—just like its counterpart, Love—is very convincing, and when it hijacks our nervous system, we are thrust into an alternate reality. Fear and its entourage of feelings like guilt, shame, and hate can creep into our lens on life and distort it, in both extreme and subtle ways. Often, the distortion is so subtle, we aren't even aware of it.

What happens if you put a drop of black ink into a glass of water? It'll instantly disperse, and ever so slightly tint everything gray. What was once clear becomes tainted. That's how fear and victim consciousness works in us; it clouds our view by distorting our lens on reality. The trick is recognizing that in those moments, we're actually in an altered state of consciousness.

Most of us live in fear as a default state that is so normalized and unconscious we never know what it actually feels like to step outside of that distorted reality and into Love. If you look at mainstream media and the stories we expose ourselves to, you'll quickly see that much of it is essentially programming us to be in a state of anxiety, judgment, and fear by perpetuating a narrative of violence, mistrust, and separation. Yet how many people in your direct, firsthand experience are actually evil? As far as we can tell, most humans we interact with radiate a sincere goodness, no matter where we travel to in the world.

When you encounter a fear pocket, the best thing to do is just to *breathe* with it. Instead of trying to fix, solve, suppress, or numb the sensation as quickly as possible, can you just give yourself the gift of witnessing the feeling in your body? Because we guarantee you, it showed up for a reason, and it has a gift for you, if you are willing to receive it.

The fear pocket can become a portal into a greater state of self-awareness, an access point to your Full Fuck Yes timeline—but it requires doing the opposite of what your fight-or-flight instinct wants you to do. In essence, you have to "*die into it*" by trusting fear to be the teacher.

Witnessing the sensation of your emotion without judgment is equivalent to wrapping that drop of ink in the protective membrane of your awareness, which Azrya likes to visualize as a white light. Becoming a loving witness to the sensation sends a signal that you are not rejecting the ink and resisting it being dropped into the glass; you're accepting it and allowing it to exist. This takes away the ink's power to muddy the rest of the water—which is a representation of your consciousness.

While this sounds simple, it's also important to remember that we are incredibly complex creatures, healing ancient wounds that are deeply embedded in our subconscious, as well as the actual cellular memory of our bodies. It takes time and dedication to move through the turbulence we've accumulated. Often, it even requires professional support.

Sometimes it might seem like the fears we are asked to face on the journey of B Ξ Q O M I N G are never-ending, but we promise you: It gets easier and easier over time.

What you'll discover is that while the turbulence feels really real, it usually passes if it's given full permission to be witnessed and expressed. And just like you aren't supposed to get up to go to the bathroom on the airplane when the Fasten Seat Belt sign comes on, we recommend you don't make any reactive decisions from the turbulent fear pocket. *Just breathe.*

Once you've allowed yourself to be with and die into it, you will discover that the sensation will evolve into something new. Sometimes "dying into it" entails the energy asking to be expressed, which can look like putting it on the page through writing, asking a friend to simply "hold space" by witnessing you as you share from your heart, allowing yourself to go into an intentional process of crying, shaking, screaming into a pillow, or blasting some tunes and dancing it out. All of these methods are highly useful in the process we call transmutation: changing the energy from one form to another.

As you become more proficient in working with your breath and your emotions, you can begin to quite literally transmute pain to pleasure, greed to generosity, and fear to love. It's an alchemical process, mastery of which is the most crucial ingredient to stabilizing in B≡QOMING Unfuckwithable.

Many of us fall in love with the idea of empowerment and transformation because we assume it's going to be a fun ride, and it absolutely is. But that doesn't mean it's not challenging as fuck sometimes. If you're anything like us, *your spirit is craving that challenge*. The thrill of pushing past your own inner edges and realizing you're actually infinitely more capable, courageous, and radiant than you could have ever dreamed of becomes not just a means to an end—it becomes a way of life.

As you deepen into this practice of facing yourself fully and leaning into the discomfort of fear over and over again, you will build tremendous trust with life, for it will constantly reward you with more love on the other side. In the beginning, when you don't have that trust yet, it can feel really fucking scary to take the first step. Trust us to KNOW that it will only ever get better if you keep following the path. In fact, after a while, there's a tipping point where you actually enjoy the thrill of finding and leaning into your next edge.

Benjamin spent years trying to find the thrill we're describing in the material realm. He got heavy into dirt bike and track racing, flew his own airplane upside down, and went skydiving and heliskiing. He did all the external, physical things to squeeze out the adrenaline of feeling fully alive in the face of potential death. But these methods were unsustainable because they always required a high-risk external circumstance to achieve the biochemical release of dopamine and adrenaline he was after, and eventually, his severe injuries forced him to find a different way to stay stimulated.

That's when he discovered that the greatest adrenaline rush is found in the richness of your own soul's untapped potential to embrace fear and expand into greater and greater depths of unimaginable Love.

The journey of B≡QOMING is not just a momentary experience that will come and go—it's a doorway to an infinite well of fascinating, tantalizing, nourishing experiences to activate within your very own DNA.

This means you get to KNOW that for the rest of your life, *it's never going to get boring.*

INVITATION #4:

- How do you experience fear in your body? What are the sensations?

- Write down at least one example of when fear prevented you from taking a risk that could have had a positive outcome.

- Write down at least one example of when you took a risk despite feeling fear. What was the outcome?

- Where is fear motivating you today?

- Where can you embrace fear as a teacher?

- Where are you justifying holding onto fear because you believe it is serving you?

- Close your eyes and consciously breathe for 10 minutes. What came up? Resistance? Distraction? Insight? Write about it.

PART 2

RELENTLESS DEVOTION

5

MEETING YOURSELF IN THE MIRROR OF LIFE

Commitment + Love = Devotion

Devotion is the cheat code to escape
the misery of self-absorption.

Azrya: I'm on the phone with an impressive clairvoyant and business coach (yes, there is such a thing), sharing my vision of global impact. Over the years, I've refined the blueprint and am now much clearer about what I'm calling in, which is funding to secure a retreat property where I can host transformational experiences for high-impact individuals and continued financing for the documentary I've begun filming. The coach offers to psychically tune into my field. I'm down. "Okay, here's what I see," she says. "You're about to meet a man who will be your game changer investor. He's ethnically diverse, and already close by."

"That's interesting," I reply while spooning almond butter out of the jar. "I wonder if I've met him. There's this guy Ben that is trying to recruit me to support his projects. He sounds like he could be who you're describing."

It's true. Ben is a Middle Eastern businessman I've recently met who is very wealthy and already working with plant medicine. On paper, he looks like he could be the ideal candidate to become my investor and ally, having just bought a gorgeous retreat center location he wants to turn into a transformational community space, with plenty of money he wants to put toward "impact investing." In our brief interactions, I could sense that he really saw me and understood what I was doing in a way few people had.

Could this be the person that I've been calling in?

Ben and I have a few more meetings to explore if I'm the right fit for a leadership role, but something isn't right. My intuition tells me to pull back. It feels like the universe is testing my ability to discern. To not be blinded by the potential but rather stop and listen to my deeper intuition. Like water circling a drain a few times before it goes in, I've come to learn that life operates in a similar way and that often **the hardest no to identify is the one closest to a yes.**

Manifestation is a journey of refinement within our own energetic signature—we get closer and closer until something just clicks. In order to find that click, though, we have to be willing to let the "almost yesses" go—even though they may be very close to what we want. Only then are we ready to receive the Full Fuck Yes.

I decide to pass on the opportunity with Ben and instead turn my attention back to dating, which is both thrilling and nerve wracking. Having been in a committed, monogamous relationship for so long, I haven't dated in a decade! Now there's Tinder and Hinge and all sorts of strange technologies that skeeve me out. So I do what I do best and keep it old school. I pull out my trusty journal, write down a powerful intention and declare it out loud to a circle of close friends:

> *Calling in Deep Soul Connection ~*
> *I am cherished and ravaged by a cosmic, primal man (not boy). This man knows himself. His body. The female body. His purpose is fully embodied. His heart, talent, and vision inspire and stimulate me mentally, emotionally, spiritually, and physically. He has anchored his gifts into the physical, aka, he's mastered the money game. His tattoos tell the story of his life.*
> *He is star power. Magnetic. He truly sees me.*
> *I melt into his silence.*

A week later, my friend Maria (who helped organize my very first Ayahuasca ceremony five years prior) happens to be in town and spontaneously invites me over to a dinner *at this guy's house who I think you should meet.*

As I park my car, I have this strange sensation that my life is about to change in a significant way.

Benjamin—"Bee"—opens the door and our eyes meet. *Oh hello.* He walks me into his sexy, sleek bachelor pad, and the first thing I see is a framed picture on the wall that says *Fuck Yes, or Fuck No.*

Instantly it's clear. I've been guided to the right place.

Bee: My first glimpse of the woman who will crack my heart wide open is of her fixing her short dark pixie hair in the reflection of the glass door. She has long, lean limbs, and her swan-like neck is adorned with black owl feathers inked into her skin.

"So tell me," she says, after we finish our dinner with Maria and the other mutual friends who introduced us. "What is your relationship to the Full Fuck Yes?"

I lean back in my seat and take a moment to reply, never taking my eyes off of her.

"The Fuck Yesses and the Fuck Nos are easy because they're obvious. It's everything in between that's hard to detect," I say, intrigued by this seemingly fearless young woman. Her smile reveals that she likes my answer.

"What about you?" I continue. "What made you realize you were qualified to coach and guide people? Did you do any formal training?"

She chuckles.

"No. I don't operate in very conventional ways," she says.

"Clearly," I reply.

"Have you ever worked with Ayahuasca?" she inquires.

"It's interesting you ask that," I reply. "I was just journaling the other day and received an intuitive hit that it's time for me to work with the medicine again. My first and only experience with Aya was seven years ago in Peru, when I was in a major transition and seeking guidance around what this next phase of my life would look like. The message I received from the medicine was a resounding *you're not ready*. This time around I sense I am ready, and the work feels like it will be an ongoing study, a deep dive into the shamanic realms."

"Ah. It makes sense we're meeting now," Azrya says with a knowing smile after I share this with her.

It doesn't take long to figure out I am a Full Fuck Yes to Azrya, although at the time I have no idea what I am getting myself into.

Azrya: This new Benjamin is more on the quiet side. His professional poker face makes it very hard for me to read him, but the energetic connection is palpable. Intrigued, I give him my number and invite him to attend a Media as Medicine group meditation ceremony called *The Cocoon Experience* that I'm hosting at The Mothership the following week. He buys a ticket and shows up in his matte gray Range Rover, wearing sunglasses, a beanie, and a burnt orange vintage tee with boobs printed on it. *Classic.* He stands out like a sore thumb, sitting in my tipi, surrounded by hippies, quietly taking it all in.

After the event ends, a small group of us goes out to lunch together. The chemistry between Benjamin and I has now become undeniable. I have this inexplicable desire to press myself right into those boobies printed on his shirt. He is so unlike anyone I've ever met. There's a deep familiarity, and at the same time, it feels like we are worlds apart. Over sushi, I can feel his eyes on me. The conversation turns to romance. I share that I'm questioning whether monogamy is an outdated model for relationships.

"What about you?" I ask Benjamin out of the blue. "Have you ever considered more of an open dynamic?"

"What did you have in mind?" he responds, calm as a cucumber. *Damn, he's good.* We laugh and he goes on to share that if he's honest with himself, he doesn't think that would be a viable option for him. "I'm more the traditional 'till death do us part' type," he explains.

Hmmm.

Later that day, my phone pings.

Bee: The next time I see you, I don't want to share you with anyone else.

Oh shit. He's officially making a move. *Eeeeeek.* Okay. I know how to do this. I decide to bounce the ball back and reply:

Az: Well, in my experience, when you ask for what you want, you might just get it...

It's on. Only thing is, I've already signed up to attend an Ayahuasca ceremony that weekend, so I can't see him again right away. On my way out of town, he texts me a couple of his Spotify playlists. The moment I slip the headphones in my ears and press play, my insides begin to melt and the sexual energy flows like warm maple syrup on Sunday morning. The music becomes a portal into his soul.

By the time I'm heading into the ceremony, my panties are soaked and all I can think about is him.

Bee: Azrya is now front and center of my awareness. I am so immersed in her energy that I am compelled to write to her. I'm not the poetic type, and even writing someone a birthday card is a stretch for me, but the moment I set pen to paper, the words just appear, almost as if they're coming from some other place.

> Dear Azrya—I see you. I see that you have felt deep pain in your life. I see that you are still uncertain. I see that you have the spirit and the eyes of a beautiful, strong, and majestic bird. I see that you have now shed the feathers that you were born with and that your wings are unbreakable. I see that you are about to soar to new heights. You will fly above us all...guiding, protecting.
>
> I don't know if we will be together for a moment or for a lifetime, but I hope that while we are together, I will be the arrow that propels you upwards.
>
> I know we will be humble teachers and grateful students to each other. I see you, my angel. I see you and I can't look away.

I sit back and read over my chicken scratch handwriting. *Did I just write that?* Considering I met this woman less than a week ago and we have never spent any time one-on-one together, the words that flowed through me shouldn't make any sense, yet somehow, they are the *only* thing that makes sense. I have no desire to play it safe, to hold back, to pretend I'm not as interested as I am. Not this time.

Our text messages get right to the point.

Bee: Do you miss me?

Az: Miss is a strong word... I'm in the inquiry around why we've been connected and how the chemistry between us may want to express itself. So you are occupying my awareness, yes.

Bee: *lol* That's a great answer.

Bee: In this weird way, I have a feeling I'm ready to show you a depth in me that I've never completely shown to anyone. And I'm surprised at how calm and knowing I feel.

Az: What an honor. The depth is all I know. I look forward to meeting you there.

Azrya: That night in ceremony, the medicine takes me straight into the most vivid visions of a shared future. Unlike any other ceremonies I have experienced, this one is intensely erotic. If you've seen Tyler Durden and Marla Singer having sex in *Fight Club*, you'll know what I mean. The visions are crisp, detailed, and graphic in their depiction of us passionately fucking, our hearts and bodies fully activated. It's like watching an explosion of juicy magic made of golden confetti, and the message from the medicine is beyond clear: *This is it. Do not hesitate. Go to him.*

The following morning, I text Benjamin:

Az: You were very present for me last night.

Bee: I'm glad to hear it. You were very present for me last night and this morning and this afternoon. How are you feeling?

I'm feeling like I've just been shown a preview for the rest of my life. Not exactly the kind of thing you share with a perfect stranger over text message. *Slow your roll, woman,* I tell myself. But at this point, there's nothing that can keep me away from him. The moment I get home, I hop in the shower, shave my aching pussy, pack an overnight bag, and drive to his house as if magnetically drawn. The gravitational pull of my body is so strong, my rational mind has absolutely no say in the situation anymore. Sitting at a stoplight, I'm flooded with a deep awareness that the woman in this car will literally not be the same come tomorrow morning.

I park outside of his house and turn the engine off. In the silence, the adrenaline coursing through my veins is much harder to ignore. Truth is, this mysterious man intimidates the shit out of me. I can sense that much of his profound depth is shrouded in shadow. There's danger here, and I like it. I take a few deep breaths, trembling with anticipation and turn-on, when the final text comes in.

Bee: The door's unlocked.

Walking in, I am so nervous I can barely make eye contact. Benjamin isn't traditionally handsome; some might even consider his look intimidating, with his bald head, deeply grooved frown lines, and dark eyes—yet he oozes sex appeal, and being in his territory sends my heart rate up a notch. My bashfulness seems to amuse him. I want to take it slow, but who am I kidding? My body is calling the shots now and food is the last thing it wants. I poke at the salmon and broccoli on my plate. Every cell in my body is alive, tingling, vibrating. It feels like I am being penetrated by his presence.

"All I know is that I don't want to rush into anything," I hear myself say, after he calmly shares with me how certain he is that something profound is about to happen between us.

"Good luck with that," he replies, without missing a beat.

I am speechless. He grins. He knows I can't resist his conviction.

About 30 minutes later I give in and melt into his warm, sturdy embrace. "Let's go upstairs," he whispers in my ear, his voice baritone silk, his scent intoxicating.

Next thing I know, I'm getting undressed. Then I'm in his bed, electricity charging through my body as our lips and skin touch for the first time. He has his way with me, making me cum hard, over and over again. The sensation of pleasure is so high-vibrational in its intensity, my entire system becomes incompatible with shame. I've never squirted like that in my life and end up drenching his entire bed. "I'm gonna start calling you 'puddles,'" he teases me. It's like we've known each other forever.

From that day forward we are inseparable, and I find myself going through a full-blown sexual awakening.

Benjamin's hands, lips, heart, and cock become my holy grail. The way that man can make me feel is unlike anything I ever imagined possible. When I was a little girl, I snuck romance novels from the library and revelled in fantasies of being "fucked open to God," as David Deida puts it, but I didn't know if those would actually ever manifest or if they were just a figment of my overactive imagination. The sex I had before I met Benjamin was wonderful. But this—this is something else.

This is a revelation.

A CLOSED HEART CAN NEVER SPEAK TRUTH

We: Why did we choose to give you the play-by-play of our meeting in such vivid detail? Because it's a story that would have never happened if we hadn't been willing to suspend our minds and open our hearts.

Bee: *Had the perfectly timed medicine ceremony not dissolved Azrya's ego and shown her that it was safe to trust me, this unknown man, layers* *of boundaries and protection mechanisms would have significantly slowed down the speed at which she moved toward me.*

Az: *If Benjamin had "played it cool," he would have waited at least a few months to see how things evolved before giving me the intimate words he channeled for me when I was still a stranger. Instead, through choosing to trust the magic of this inexplicable connection, he vulnerably exposed himself and gave me the handwritten card the morning after our first night together.*

We: Neither of us would have been willing to take these kinds of risks if we had listened to the defense mechanisms protecting our hearts. And yet, it is exactly the willingness to take these types of risks that are a prerequisite for living a rich and magical life.

If we truly want to live from a place of love rather than fear, first we must examine the condition our hearts are in. What we'll find is fairly shocking. Our hearts have closed in ways we aren't even aware of.

Why? Because the world we've lived in has not been safe to feel.

If the heart is the night club, the ego is the overzealous bouncer. It deflects anything at the door that it thinks might ruin the vibe of the party. You might argue that this is a valuable thing, and protects the integrity of the inner space, but unfortunately, our bouncers/egos are operating from the illusion of separation, which keeps them in tunnel vision, obsessed with looking for potential dangers or threats that could lead to emotional pain. They are so suspicious of incoming, unknown energies that they often end up killing the party.

By being unwilling to risk deep feeling, the heart atrophies like a muscle that isn't used. The irony is, the weaker it grows, the more easily bruised, wounded, and broken it becomes. Once that has happened a few times, the scar tissue that builds up energetically around the heart adds yet another boundary of protection to the already starving heart, and the bouncer becomes even more vigilant. It's a vicious cycle, and the only way to break it is to begin—layer by layer—to dissolve the scar tissue around the heart and slowly but surely educate the bouncer until he becomes a trustworthy guardian, not a brute force of blind rejection.

A closed heart is not only deeply tragic; it is also dangerous, for it deflects and projects hurt and heartbreak onto others in a desperate attempt not to feel its own pain. When you look at the state of the world, especially interpersonal relationships, you can see this play itself out with dire consequences. With so much scar tissue creating distortions and interferences in the language our hearts speak, we cannot trust them to recognize and communicate truth, which is a very scary way to live. Our most powerful compass with which to navigate the complex reality of the human experience is compromised.

We will not evolve if we do not learn to open our hearts and feel again. That requires us revisiting all of the past hurts we've collected as scar tissue around our hearts. It's a tender and beautiful process that takes time, patience, and excruciating honesty.

THE DOJO OF RELATIONSHIPS

Our most intimate relationships are the greatest catalyst for quantum growth because we often attract people who are an exact match to some of our deepest fears, insecurities, and core woundings (as you'll see, we—Az and Bee—are not exempt). It's almost like our soul curriculum was perfectly designed to push, activate, and trigger the exact buttons that lead us to the most challenging (and rewarding) exams.

The more committed to B ≡ Q O M I N G each person is, the greater the chances of that relationship thriving, because the masks that create disconnection or staleness are constantly coming off to reveal the truth underneath, mirrored back through the eyes of the beloved. Is being on a path of personal transformation the ultimate guarantee that your relationship will last forever, no matter what? No. Life is full of surprises, twists, and turns. Certain relationships are not meant to last forever. There's a difference between being committed and being attached. Sometimes the loss of a loved one, through a breakup, divorce, or even death, can be the greatest catalyst for expansion. *As much as we get to commit, we also get to develop the discernment to KNOW when it's time to go all in and when it's time to let go.* But if we do let go, let us let go in love instead of fear.

It's easy to underestimate just how much of our reality is shaped by relationships. You simply can't avoid them. Even beyond your spouse, friends, family, and colleagues, you are in relationship with your health, your finances, your mechanic, and the universe at large.

If you look at the common denominator between all relationships, you'll find that they all require feeling to function. It's hard to be truly intimate with anyone or anything if your emotions are on lock down. Therefore, the more in tune with your feelings you are and the more mastery over your emotions (and subsequent emotional signature) you have, the more intentionally you can navigate relationships and thus shape the very fabric of your reality.

Out of all of the things we could be teaching our children in school, navigating the complex terrain of relationships would undoubtedly be one of the most valuable. It is at the very root of what makes us human, and yet, it is almost always completely overlooked; a glaring blind spot within our culture.

MASCULINE / FEMININE ENERGIES

Everything in the universe exists on a spectrum of opposites. Love and fear, light and dark, north and south, hot and cold, day and night, sun and moon, yin and yang. We are no different. Every human, regardless of gender, has both masculine and feminine energies within them.

In *The Way of the Superior Man*, David Deida describes it like this: "Like a ship cutting through a vast ocean, the masculine decides on a course and navigates the direction: the feminine energy itself is undirected but immense, like the wind and deep currents of the ocean, ever-changing, beautiful, destructive, and the source of life."

The masculine (Alpha) holds the container which you can think of as a riverbed; it provides the direction and structure that the feminine waters, the river of creative life-force energy, can flow freely within. Another metaphor is the masculine as the drumbeat and the feminine as the melody. The masculine is usually associated with informing the world of form and is linear thinking and freedom-driven, whereas the feminine (Omega) is usually associated with matter (Mother Earth), intuitive feeling, and being love-driven. To overgeneralize, you could say the masculine aims to penetrate life and the feminine aims to be penetrated by life.[2] Because these energies exist on opposite poles, there is a tension that is created between them, which can be experienced as sexual attraction or creative synergy. It's the spark that gives birth to babies and projects. The greater the polarity, the greater the magnetic pull between opposites. In some dynamics, men hold more feminine energy than women and vice versa. It doesn't actually matter what gender you identify with; as long as you have polarity, you will balance each other out and create dynamic tension.

Different levels of activation or suppression of the masculine and feminine energies inform our identity. A fully integrated being can dance and flow between them (and discover many more that we don't even have names for yet), but most people are lopsided. Fear, control, greed, and lust create enslavement and distortion. We must shine the light of awareness upon the traumatized aspects of these energies before we can get to the healthy expression of them. Our world is ready for consciousness to revolutionize how masculine

2   Inspired by Justin Patrick Pierce.

and feminine energy occurs within each and every human being, but we must first liberate ourselves from the wounding and war that has occurred between these polarities, as they have played themselves out in vicious cycles of victim/perpetrator loops for thousands of years.

To live in a state of liberation is to live in a state of acceptance, celebration, and love—of ourselves and our opposites. Only when we clear the baggage of the past by truly embracing the full spectrum of light and shadow contained within the masculine and feminine will these energies mature into the embodiment of the benevolent King/Queen archetypes, who can act as pillars to communities and societies at large.

WHAT ARE YOU WILLING TO RISK FOR FULL ALIVENESS?

When you watch *Planet Earth* or the Discovery Channel and see cheetahs prowling the savannah or nebulae painting masterpieces in the galaxy, are you reminded of the vast complexity, intricacy, and creativity of the universe? Are you awed by the intense and constant interplay between the forces of life and death, perpetrator and prey, beauty and pain?

How about when you look into your own eyes in the mirror. Do you see the cosmic potential of your own being staring back at you? Do you feel that same sense of awe and wonder at your own mysterious, multidimensional nature, or are you taking yourself for granted?

Embracing the full spectrum of yourself is crucial if you wish to cultivate the deepest levels of intimacy with anyone else. Why? Because it's where you train yourself to become attuned to the nuances of sensation that arise as you push past your own internal edges. As you stretch past your comfort zone and engage more deeply with your own inner world, you'll find the highs get higher and the lows get lower, and in turn, your capacity to become a vessel for intimacy and magic increases because there's simply more energy that's able to move through you.

For example: Imagine a woman who is having a really hard time expressing pleasure vocally during sex with her husband. She just can't seem to relax into the experience—her head keeps getting in the way. Were she to decide to address the root cause, she might uncover that there's a layer of suppressed rage that she never expressed from when she was taken advantage of by her first boyfriend. That rage has been so scary to feel she's squashed it down to the point where it's now literally creating an energetic block in her throat. Subconsciously, she's afraid that if she lets her voice fully express, this rage will be unleashed at her husband and she'll freak him out! She's not wrong. Sound (and orgasm) can unlock all sorts of emotion stored in the body; that's why it's such a powerful healing modality. But if the woman can start to consciously work with the energy, she can express and release it fully in a safe space outside of the bedroom and be much more free to emote during sex. This is what it looks like to literally embrace the full spectrum of who you are, and on the other side, more of your magic is available to be shared.

When we use the word "magic," we're not talking about card trick magic, by the way. We're talking about getting out of the way so that the infinitely imaginative and playful forces of the universe can work through you and align the circumstances and events of your daily life in a way that becomes ever increasingly pleasurable and profound. Some call this flow state. Others call it synchronicity. Call it what you will, once you get a taste, you'll never want to go back because the menu of life just got a whole lot richer.

The path of B Ξ Q O M I N G demands that you meet yourself fully and unapologetically in the mirror of life. Without embracing the full spectrum of your raw, uncensored nature, you will never be able to cultivate the depth of trust necessary to truly KNOW yourself as a powerful co-creator of your reality. You must understand the components and the parts that you're made of first, before you can begin to productively use them to create magic.

Look at yourself in the mirror as if you were watching The Discovery Channel. Give yourself the greatest gift there is: your full presence. Feel the blood pumping in your veins. As Brad Pitt's famous character Tyler Durden says in *Fight Club*, "this is your *life* and it's ending one minute at a time." Can you make contact with your primal nature, the part of you that remembers how to fight, fuck, and feast, the part of you that KNOWS how to have a passionate love affair with the terrifying beauty of what it means to be truly alive?

If not, *that's okay.* We have spent most of our lives living in mental prisons, squashing our emotions and chasing imaginary finish lines, so it's no wonder we've become desensitized to our primal nature. Embracing the fullness of who you are also includes embracing the parts of you that have perhaps become suspicious of life or domesticated to the point of feeling somewhat numb. It means slowing down to embrace the parts that are absolutely terrified of meeting yourself fully. Giving our Truest Truth a voice requires understanding which parts of us are in resistance to embracing all that we are and acknowledging where our hearts are closed due to fear, trauma, or conditioning. It is only through the integration of these soul "fragments" that we B ≡ Q O M ≡ able to say a whole-hearted *Fuck Yes* to life. Armed with the KNOWING that all of life is conspiring to support you in delivering precisely the soul curriculum you require to B ≡ Q O M ≡ your most magnetic and magnificent self, you now stand at the threshold to new dimensions of expansion and experience.

Remember, the ego wants to control. The soul wants to surrender.

You are being invited to stand on the edge of the cliff and claim your place in this world.

Are you ready to allow the universe to illuminate *everything you didn't know you wanted*?

Are you ready to consciously surrender to life and let yourself be held by the great mystery?

We promise you, it's safe to let go.

INVITATION #5:

- When you look in the mirror of your soul, what do you see? What do you feel?

- Where is your heart closed to yourself or others? Is it protecting you from feeling pain?

- Where does your ego prevent you from deeper intimacy with self and others?

- Who do you currently love with an open heart? Spouse, kids, family, friends, animals, plants, planet? What does it feel like?

- If you were to CLAIM your heart's desires and embrace more of yourself - how would your life be different?

- Pick someone who you have guarded or closed your heart towards and write them a letter. (This could also be yourself.) You don't have to give it to them, but practice letting the words penetrate your heart and open it, consciously aiming love towards this person.

6

EMBRACE THE WAVES
YOUR TRUTH MAKES

"Those who failed to oppose me...who readily
agreed with me and accepted all my views...
were those who did me the most injury."

—N. B.

Azrya: Being freshly in love is extremely energizing, awe-inspiring, profoundly magical, and also really fucking intense. Benjamin and I are worlds colliding, and our two extremely strong personalities with well-established worldviews are merging at a rapid rate. Within the first two weeks, it quickly becomes apparent that we're aligned beautifully in pretty much every area except for two. Both of which have the potential to be serious deal breakers.

"I've never believed in marriage, and I have questions about monogamy," I share with Benjamin one evening as we sit outside at a restaurant, stealing bites from each other's plates. "I guess I just wonder if these are outdated paradigms for relationships. If we can evolve past needing guarantees to feel safe, learn to truly trust life, and let go of shame, jealousy, and insecurity, why would we require a model for relationships that limits love in any way or locks us into decisions about a future that we can't possibly control?"

I can feel him contract as I speak. The truth of my questioning has disturbed him.

The next day, he calls me while I'm on a hike.

"Listen," he says, his voice heavy. "I've been really sitting with what you said last night, and I have to be honest, it's raising a lot of red flags for me. I've been very clear from the beginning that what I'm looking for is commitment. I'm calling in The One. I don't want to continue opening my heart to you if that's not where you're at. Maybe we're not meeting at the right time. Maybe you need to get some stuff out of your system and call me in a year. I don't know, but I don't want to keep going down this path if we're fundamentally misaligned."

My eyes well with tears. The idea of this connection fizzling out before it's even really gotten started feels like a punch in the gut. At the same time, the fear of breaking his heart down the road because I wasn't fully honest up front rears its ugly head. I take a few deep breaths, the emotion tightening my throat.

"I'm going to hang up and cry, *a lot*," I tell him calmly. "Then I'll call you back."

I end the call, sink to the earth, wrap my arms around my knees, and sob for a solid five minutes. *How is it possible that I already love this man so much the idea of losing him is devastating?* I calm down and recenter. We're at a choice point. Telling him what he wants to hear by pretending I'm someone I'm not isn't an option. But I can't not fight for this love.

"I hear you," I say, after I call him back. "And I guess all I can say is this: I don't presume to have any solid answers, nor do I know what's true for me around relationships right now. I've been in monogamous relationships for most of my adult life, the last one lasting almost a decade, and you're the first person I've connected with since. What I do know for sure is that what we have is crazy special and every part of me wants to keep leaning into it."

"So what are you saying?" he asks.

"I'm inviting you to trust," I reply.

He does. The next day, we fly to Tulum to attend the Summit conference. As our connection deepens, so does my desire to commit. The night of our LSD journey seals the deal. After being blindfolded, tied up, and ravished, I write the following poem in my journal:

> *Little did I know how much I was craving to be ravished*
> *To be claimed*
> *To be devoured*
> *My body bound*
> *My spirit unchained*

A Queen needs a King
Let it be proclaimed

I'm as All In as I know how to be.

Then comes the second roadblock. During a sound bath meditation we're attending at our resort, I make contact with the part of me that desires to be a mother. The feeling is beautiful, heart expansive, and tender—and yet it also feels heartbreaking because Benjamin has shared with me that he doesn't want any more children. His decision is final and solidified by the fact that he got a vasectomy 13 years prior, after his son—who is on the autism spectrum—was born, and who he struggles to connect with. I feel the conflicting energy of my profound love for Benjamin collide with the potential timeline of bringing life into this world. I reach over and squeeze his hand, his warmth spilling into my body, sending tears to my eyes.

After the meditation is over, we lay outside on the balcony of our casita, listening to the ocean lap against the shore, his head resting on my chest. I vulnerably share with him what came up.

"I thought you said you weren't attached to having kids," he says.

"I'm not attached," I reply. "It's very possible that it's not meant to happen in this lifetime, and I'm okay with that. But I can't deny that there is a part of me that does have the desire, and it would feel out of integrity to withhold that from you because that desire could one day grow."

He's silent. Once again, I can feel the impact of my words.

Oh, the ripples that our truth makes.

"Okay," he says. "I guess all we can do is trust, right?"

"That's right," I say. And hold him tight.

I am talking about trusting in the universe's plan for us. Only much later does it become clear that he's talking about trusting that I will not want to have a child.

Despite the fact that we are unknowingly on different pages, the energy of trust melts our fear. The next day on our way to dinner, Benjamin stops suddenly, his eyes lighting up. "I just had a vision of us building a retreat center together," he says. I feel the Full Fuck Yes send shivers down my spine. "Let's do it," I say with a grin spreading from ear to ear.

That night at dinner, we begin planning our lives together. It becomes glaringly obvious that our unique backgrounds and diverse gifts perfectly complement each other and that we can combine them into a shared purpose. We have endless hours of conversations, interrupted only by ravenous love making and epic meals under whispering palm trees. It feels like we're on our honeymoon, not like we met three weeks ago.

Then it's time to go home. On the plane, I begin writing what will eventually become the seed of this book. The words flow through me effortlessly, fueled by the electric power of our chemistry.

We arrived in Tulum as individuals, love drunk on potential. We return to LA as a unit, fully anchored into a merged future.

Four months later, I'm standing upstairs in the master bedroom of the new home Benjamin and I manifested together. Nestled in a lush canyon just 10 minutes from the ocean and flanked by miles and miles of state park, it has everything from giant sycamores to ancient oaks. Butterflies, hummingbirds, owls, and hawks coexist amongst blossoms and branches. The property is spacious enough to comfortably host our future retreat guests and the occasional mountain lion or coyote that jumps the fence.

Today though, the California sky is unusually gray and raindrops speckle the window pane as I watch cars pull into the driveway below. What the people in those cars don't know is that they are not here to attend a housewarming party. They are here to attend what has evolved into a surprise wedding.

When exactly did Benjamin and I decide to spend the rest of our lives together? I can't remember. It's almost like we never actually made a conscious choice. Instead, it feels more like the Choiceless Choice that was there from the moment we spent that first night together, five months ago to the day.

And now here we are. Living together on our dream property, about to shock the shit out of 80 of our closest friends and family by baring our souls. Despite how much we love each other and how excited we are for this moment, truth is, we are both pretty fucking stressed out. And no wonder. We moved into this house less than a month ago, unpacked, went to Burning Man for a week, partied like rockstars, came home covered in sparkles and Nevada desert dust, continued to unpack, flew in a tattoo artist from Hungary to live with us and work on us extensively, and amidst all of that, organized our surprise wedding in three weeks without any support. On top of that, my mother is visiting from Switzerland and meeting Benjamin and his family for the first time, and most of the people who are coming today have no context for the massive life decisions and quantum leaps we've made together. While it might seem crazy to take all of that on, it truly did all emerge from the blueprint of our Full Fuck Yes timeline, although at one point the stress gets so intense, we almost call it off. But that doesn't want to happen. The momentum of our love is pushing us through the intensity, like a mother pushing through the contractions.

This is why you'd normally have a bridal party, I realize. *So they can emotionally support you during this rite of passage, cause it's kind of a big deal.*

Right.

Except of course, I'm the kind of person who insists on not playing by the rules. So here I am, all alone upstairs, wearing a simple, floor-length cotton dress from Tulum, about to make a lifetime commitment to a man I am technically still just getting to know, and the intensity of what's about to come is building up in my nervous system. I don't know most of the people Benjamin has invited, and I can already feel that many of them will not know what to make of me. Through their lens, I am likely going to appear like a massive glitch in the matrix.

The rain isn't helping. Our entire event is outside, and we still haven't been able to set up the Moroccan rugs and pillows that our guests will sit on under a large tent, where we plan to share the play-by-play of our love story with them. This approach seemed more efficient than trying to catch everyone up individually. Not even Benjamin's mother or children know what's going to come after we give everyone the backstory. While we've both agreed that we don't need a piece of paper to validate our love and we are essentially "marrying" ourselves, the energetics of this ceremony are significant and, in many ways, totally out of my comfort zone.

Here we grow.

I take a deep breath and go downstairs to find three of my dearest soul sisters in the kitchen, stirring a large pot of liquid. Oh yeah, I forgot to mention that part. We've decided to offer everyone magic mushroom tea, because why not throw a psychedelic journey into the mix to keep things interesting?

Right before we're about to begin the official part of the event, it stops raining. As everyone mingles, Benjamin pulls me aside. "Come over here with me." He gestures toward a bench, away from the people. We sit under Wisteria vines climbing wood, their lavender blossoms hanging over us like bunches of grapes. The moment it's just me and him, I feel my whole body relax. He is my energetic docking station. In his presence, I am home. *This is why I said yes to all of this craziness*, I remember, trying to breathe deeply. *Because it's him.*

"You ready to rock this, big momma?" he asks. He gave me that nickname right when we met, and somehow it's stuck to my 110-pound frame like glue.

I nod. "Show me the way." He grins and takes my small hand in his large one. We make our way back to our unsuspecting guests and invite everyone to take a seat. Once those who choose to participate have received their cup of mushroom tea, we ask everyone to close their eyes, connect with the spirit of the medicine and the land and set their intention. Then we begin.

Bee: "We've called you all together because we want to share with you how we got here and how we intend to activate this land," I announce to the many faces looking Azrya and me.

The crowd includes an eclectic mix of my CEO peers, bros from when I was a kid, blood family, and Azrya's shamanic, tattooed, conscious community. Going into this experience, I know it's going to take a lot of finesse to try and bridge the gap between where everyone is at and pierce through potential judgment so they can understand the depth of this love. Like trying to merge many opposing flavors into a cohesive dish, the task feels daunting and has given me a fair amount of anxiety. But I know that all I can do is speak from the heart and give everyone who is willing an opportunity to join Azrya and me on this shared journey. The rest is beyond my control.

"We didn't finalize the name for this property until 7 a.m. this morning," I continue. "Azrya came downstairs holding a copy of David Brooks's book, *The Second Mountain*, which we read together when we were first falling in love in Tulum. David's concept perfectly captures the pivot from chasing profit on the First Mountain to living with purpose on the Second Mountain. As many of you know, that's the pivot I've been seeking for many years. It also accurately describes the journey we want to guide high-impact individuals through with the transformational work we will be facilitating here on this property. So, we welcome you to our home, now officially named The Second Mountain."

At this point, the mushrooms are starting to kick in, and they're about five times stronger than we anticipated. "Holy shit," I say, squinting at the notes in my hands, "the words are melting off the page!" Everyone laughs.

"This was a good idea," Azrya assures me, cracking up. "This was a very good idea."

We end up talking for an hour and a half, taking the crowd on a journey through our fairy tale romance—including reading our first text messages and journal entries aloud while sharing the full spectrum of our connection, fears, doubts, and medicine work.

While 80 percent of the attendees are riveted and hanging onto every word, I can also viscerally feel the dissonance in the space. Some of my friends are either checked out or exchanging glances and eye rolls while looking increasingly uncomfortable at the depth of vulnerability and uncensored display of emotion. Surely, they are wondering why this housewarming party has become such a love fest, and why we're talking so damn much.

This is what I was anticipating, and it's taking everything I've got to stay present with the beauty of this moment while I process the conflicting energy of worlds colliding. It's not easy to break the mold and follow your truth, especially when that truth challenges the heart of the status quo, and you're declaring your love for a woman whose friends check all of the boxes of the hippy stereotype—while on magic mushrooms!

"So, when are you guys gonna get married?" our friend Adrian calls out at the end of our talk with his thick Australian accent. He's one of the few who's in on it.

"How about now?" I respond. Everyone laughs, then quickly quiets down as I stand up, my demeanor reverent. *Oh shit, this is serious.*

It's time.

"My name is Benjamin Bequer, son of Leyda Bequer, son of Ben Bequer, ex-husband of Grisel Bequer and father of Gysel and Steel Bequer.

"Mom, Grisel, Gysel, Steel..." I address each member of my family. "Will you please stand." They do. One by one, I ask if they will accept Azrya into the family. A hush falls over the crowd. Everyone is starting to realize what this is. Each family member agrees. Gysel bursts into tears.

"I have a question for this woman that she's not expecting." I announce. Then I turn to Azrya and reach for her hand. At this point everyone is probably thinking we're about to get engaged. Nope. We're already at the altar.

"Will you take my last name?" I have tears in my eyes.

Azrya is visibly flooded with emotion. Placing one hand on her heart she says, "It would be an honor."

Elated, I address the crowd. "I would like to introduce you to my wife...Azrya Bequer."

We lock lips and the crowd erupts in celebration. From that moment forward, everything is a blur. We are bombarded with hugs and well-wishes from every direction. Tears and mescal flow freely. The DJ turns up the music. All the stress from the previous four weeks melts away.

We did it.

We threw all caution to the wind and anchored in our shared future.

Little do we know the immensity of the soul curriculum we just said "I do" to.

TO CENSOR OR NOT TO CENSOR?

Azyra: I pull up a photo of me passionately kissing a woman and stare at it.

As I allow the image to evoke the feeling of her soft-as-silk lips in my memory, I replay the beautiful way in which Mars became a welcome addition to mine and Benjamin's union.

Since I was 13, I have always been attracted to women, but never had the courage to act on it. Mars had been a friend on my B Ξ Q O M I N G path for a while, and there was deep trust already established, so when I initiated for the dynamic between the three of us to become intimate, it felt seamless and organic. Not a shred of jealousy, insecurity, or fear has been steering the ship.

There are no labels to define this little love triangle, but that doesn't make it casual. There's a sacredness to our connection, a healing energy that is generated when we are together. At the core of our choice to share our bodies with each other in an intentional, reverent way is a genuine, deep love that only strengthens over time.

Benjamin and I believe in the power of transparency. Once we agree to openly share about our relationship with Mars in this book as part of our chapter on sexuality, we know it's time to tell the family. The next time Bee's mom, ex-wife Grisel, and 19-year-old daughter Gysel are all together, we come out of the closet and soon find this nourishing source of intimacy, play, and pleasure tainted by a very sobering reality.

Suffice it to say, the conversation doesn't go well.

Now, Grisel is on her way over to have a heart-to-heart with me, one-on-one.

She arrives, and I sit down across from her, feeling knots in her stomach as if they were my own. This is a huge-hearted woman who I deeply respect and love, who I've sat in Ayahuasca ceremonies with, and who is looking at me now with distress in her soulful dark eyes.

"I'm having a very hard time understanding how you could put the sacredness of your marriage in such jeopardy—and on top of that, share it publicly," she says, on the verge of tears. "I just don't see how it could bring anything but harm."

Since the beginning, Grisel has been a cheerleader for me coming into the tight-knit family unit and has celebrated us in our union and encouraged my connection with the kids. In fact, it was Grisel who gifted us printed jewelry boxes with our pictures on it that said "A + B Unfuckwithable" as her wedding gift.

Now she's come to me, not with judgment, but with a genuine desire to understand and voice her fears around how this would affect—and possibly threaten—the well-being of the family. The core of her concern is coming from a deep love for Benjamin and me—although it is being filtered—and thus distorted—through a lens of fear. Fear of the family unit being weakened. Fear of feathers getting ruffled. Fear of Benjamin and I making an irreversible mistake and jeopardizing our shared future. Fear of what kind of example we are setting for the kids.

All valid concerns—of course. But embedded with fear nonetheless.

During the deeply authentic conversation that follows, my innately radical, punk poet, medicine woman, trailblazing, truth-seeking, textbook aquarian self, who lives in a country that prides itself on freedom of speech and "liberty for all," finds herself puzzled by how exactly to respond to what feels like a distorted interpretation of what Benjamin, Mars, and I have been experiencing as so pure.

"It feels like I am being told the way in which I love is not okay and must be censored or hidden in some way," I reflect to Grisel, trying to not sound defensive. I am struggling to understand how I can avoid disrespecting values instilled by a widely accepted rule book governing a love-deprived society while still remaining true to myself. It feels like a stalemate.

I ask Grisel to consider that the energy between me, Benjamin, and Mars has all of the qualities she would associate with a healthy expression of love: blissful, natural, expansive, inspiring, healing, compassionate, playful, easeful. Anyone who has ever been in love and touched such high frequencies knows how enriching and nourishing it is to bask in the stream of energy that love unlocks between open hearts and willing bodies. In fact, without love, life loses its meaning entirely.

"So why then, for something most would agree belongs to the most cherished experience on Earth, should love be stifled or made secret when all participating parties are in full choice and following their sovereign, Full Fuck Yes?" I ask her.

"What if it turns sour?" Grisel responds. "What if someone gets hurt?"

Love does often hurt, doesn't it, especially when sex is involved. That's why we arm ourselves against the very thing we crave most. Because love can crack us open, and it can shatter us apart. Love and sex are forces of nature that can't be controlled, only stewarded. To steward instead of control is to trust in something bigger than you. It's to trust in the unknown. And it's scary AF.

Maybe that's why, the moment we are born, we get imprinted with the societally approved versions of love and sex, which exist in very tiny boxes, of which there are few to choose from. These boxes dictate the "appropriate" way to love and "make love," which varies depending on culture or religious beliefs. *If I just stay in the box, then I'll be safe to love*, we naively think, just as if it were our idea. *If I just stay in the box, I have control.*

But love doesn't give a fuck about boxes. If it did, divorce rates wouldn't be at over 40 percent. Love goes where it needs to go. We can guide it, we can honor it, we can dig deep and heal the parts of us that subconsciously want to sabotage it—but we cannot control love because it doesn't belong to us. It is a gift from the great mystery of life itself. A gift so profound it has compelled humanity to form deep-seated values and belief systems around it, many of which clash and contradict each other to the point where love turns in on itself and becomes infected with its polarity: fear.

I feel very clear that an integral part of my legacy is to liberate love from the clutches of fear, and to do so by providing a lived example. But Grisel is making me realize that the decision to bring Mars into our hearts and bedroom and share that information publicly with the world is going to shape not only our legacy but also the legacy of the entire family. Through her questions, she helps me see the responsibility in the creative power Benjamin and I wield. It's not just about us anymore. Our truth has consequences that will ripple into the lives of others, and our definition of love isn't in resonance with those we care about, nor will it be with many of our readers.

The conversation with Grisel ends on a positive note. She allows her guard down enough to let my perspective penetrate hers, and I do the same. We embrace and part ways, both digesting the perspective of the other.

The conversation I have with Benjamin's mother the following week is not quite as productive. I can feel her contraction simply from being in my presence. She hears the words I am saying, but they're not resonating. Her mind is made up.

"Look," she says finally, "what you and Benjamin do behind closed doors is your business, I don't have to approve. But please. *Don't write about it in the book.* If not for me, then for the sake of preserving the kids' reputation."

I feel for her. Her family is her legacy, and here I am, tarnishing it by insisting on going against the grain. I leave her house with a heavy heart.

Is the most loving choice to remain silent for once? I wonder to myself as I'm hiking the trail behind The Second Mountain the following day. *Am I being selfish for insisting on waving my "freak flag" high?*

As I watch the wind ripple through the long grasses under a cloud-less sky, my former client turned soul ally, Anáil, floats into my awareness, with a sweet reminder.

When we first met, Anáil was a housewife from Connecticut, with four kids nearing college age, a healthy business, and a marriage void of romance that had been arranged by her Indian family when she was far too young and eager to please to even consider saying no. An empath and a mystic by nature, she had always been drawn to spirituality and the healing arts but didn't see herself as a healer, and so she threw herself into the pre-prescribed role her culture had defined for her. When Anáil discovered that I selectively inte-grated psilocybin mushrooms into my coaching work, she had a dream that the medicine was calling her toward her truth. Despite her family's vehement disapproval and belief that she was being led astray, she made the leap out of her comfort zone, got on a plane, and experienced her first altered state, ever.

During the journey, I guided Anáil through layers of paralyzing fear around owning her truth and the quaking it would create in her life. To speak to her fear, I wrote on a note card *"Embrace the waves your truth makes"* and handed it to her. Something clicked. From that day forward, she was never the same. She has since taken on the role of a spiritual mentor and has been facilitating psilocybin ceremonies for her mentees. Her husband has become her greatest ally, and her friends and family have recognized the depth of her powerful transformation. She is living her most authentic truth with a finger on the pulse of her purpose. But first, she had to take the leap of faith, and get comfortable with ruffling the feathers of her entire reality. She had to break the mold and risk it all.

Over the years, I've coached countless individuals to learn to celebrate their Truest Truth without inhibition, and what I've seen over and over again is that it demands sacrifice.

The sacrifice is comfortability. We must be willing to ruffle feathers, often of those we love most. We must be willing to break out of the narrow boxes that attempt to define our multidimensional selves, even if it hurts. We cannot shy away from the difficult conversations; we must face them with an open heart. If we are willing to do that with self-responsibility, compassion, and integrity, then those who are truly meant to be in our life will respect us for it, and those who are not will fall away.

In order for us to evolve and create the kind of change our planet is so desperately crying out for, we've got to be willing to get uncomfortable. Firmly cemented belief systems and values must be shaken loose, outdated paradigms must crumble, unsustainable systems must collapse, limitations must be dissolved, and new ways must be embraced.

I've devoted years of deep inner work to discover my Truest Truth, and then more inner work to own and speak it freely without shame. But the impulse to make myself small in order to put others at ease still faintly echoes, I realize, standing on that mountain top, especially when it comes to family—a family whose approval and warmth I crave, having never really had a family unit of my own. I find compassion for that part of me, the one who wants to play the part of the "good wife" and who still cares what others think, because she *cares*. Period.

I let her know that I acknowledge her fear, but I'm going to do this anyway.

It's not going to be easy, I tell her. *But it's the only thing that's True.*

Bee: "Why do you think Dad got pancreatic cancer?" I ask my mother on Christmas Eve. We are having a face-to-face after a turbulent year, during which my life choices with Azrya have triggered a strong resistance within her.

"I don't know, maybe all the stress," she replies.

"Exactly," I say. "The stress, the scarcity, the anxiety. Dad subconsciously manifested that cancer because he never addressed the root cause of his mental and emotional health. Not long ago, I was on the same trajectory."

I'm trying to explain to her why I am so dedicated to the plant medicine path, but ever since she found out about Mars and started to tell the rest of the family that she was no longer coming to our house, the energy hasn't felt right between us.

My mother is a vivacious, caring, and deeply traditional woman who had me when she was just 19 years old and is extremely devoted to our family. We have a beautiful relationship and I love her deeply, so it's painful to feel my personal choices related to the plant medicines and Mars threatening our bond. Truthfully, part of the reason she's struggling so much to understand me is because she doesn't feel like I've shown up for my son Steel the way a father with a special needs child should and that I'm prioritizing my personal development over connecting more deeply with him.

She's not wrong.

The dynamic between Steel and I has been one of my greatest challenges and it's taken a lot of maturing for me to realize that, due to the path of navigating his special needs, Steel has been my greatest teacher. What my mom doesn't see is that a huge intention fueling all of my personal development work is to B Ξ Q O M Ξ the father he deserves. It is humbling to admit that I need help to get there. Although I want to be in surrendered acceptance of her reaction to my life choices, I am struggling to not take it personally.

I want her to support me on my path of B Ξ Q O M I N G. I am desperate for her to understand it's not an easy one.

In this situation, the old me—who had a tendency to control and manipulate—would have tried to convince, coerce, and explain myself to her until I was blue in the face. But I'm changing, learning to *respond rather than react*, so I decide to take a step back instead. As I really sit with it and put myself in her shoes, I realize: The best way I can love her right now is not by trying to fix the situation or force her to understand me, but rather to simply give myself and her space by giving us both "the privilege of our process," as our friend Briana says.

Sometimes the things we want most from others are the things we aren't willing to give.

I want her to understand me. So where am I refusing to understand her?

Past my own ego's attachments to being right, I can see how disorienting my recent transformation must be for her. She has no reference point for so much of what I'm devoting myself to. On top of that, she's seen me go all in to things really quickly, which has sometimes bitten me in the ass pretty dramatically.

Perhaps her lack of trust in my maturity and discernment to know that this path is not just a "phase" but rather a fundamental way of life is a reflection of my own subconscious doubts that I am still processing as I stabilize in greater and greater trust. I've always been an extreme guy, but it's a lot easier to be a trailblazer when those around you are cheering you on. As long as I was playing by the rules of consensus reality, speeding up the First Mountain of traditional success and acquiring more and more material wealth, I was deeply supported, even admired.

But now that I'm going in the other direction for the first time, my choices are creating a painful tension between me and those I care most about, as became obvious during the surprise union ceremony. Instead of things smoothing out over time, the friction seems to be increasing. My mother and my childhood best friend Jay—who I've known since first grade—have become two of the greatest naysayers.

"I don't see Ayahuasca being any different than snorting cocaine or shooting heroin," Jay—a former drug addict—goes off on me while we're out at dinner. "I'm genuinely worried about you, bro. Your dad would be so disappointed if he was here. You're setting a terrible example for your kids."

Wow. Remember that thing I said about responding versus reacting? This is one of those times where that's really hard.

I remind myself, *Trust the triggers to teach.*

"Jay," I *respond*, trying to stay calm while my blood boils. "I feel more blessed, at peace, and fulfilled than I ever have in my entire life. After years of searching, I've found the woman of my dreams. I am burning with the desire to have a positive impact on the planet and I'm finally shedding the weight of stress and lack that I've been carrying around for decades. Does that mean nothing to you?"

He stares at me blankly.

It's irrelevant.

No part of him is trying to understand my choices, nor the extraordinarily positive impact those choices are having on my internal state. He is much more committed to judging them. He is committed to being right. Through the lens of confirmation bias, all of my explanations fall flat. You can't argue with ignorance.

I believe the opposite of learning is knowing.

As I reflect on the dinner later that night, I realize that with Jay being his usual "all knowing" self and projecting all of his past experiences from being a drug addict onto me, I could have just sat there and been amused at how little grasp he has of the beauty and profundity of my life. But I let it get to me. I let him get under my skin. I allowed his close-mindedness to trigger me, and so I began defending myself and justifying why I was doing the things I was doing. I was trying to explain something to someone who had no interest in understanding—a frustrating endeavor and a dead end.

The emotional turmoil doesn't subside instantly. It takes me a while to process what happened and, indeed, grieve the reality that my oldest friend can't accompany me on this leg of my B≡QOMING journey. The old me would have wallowed in resentment and anger for months, but the new me has no interest in holding onto any of that.

I am amazed at how quickly I am able to bounce back once I look within, feel what I have to feel, take full ownership over my triggers, and then let it all go. I even resist the urge to reach out and initiate a follow-up conversation where I might have another chance of explaining myself. In the end, I simply text Jay and let him know that I love him. Because I do, whether he agrees with me or not. We are brothers for life, and no matter what he throws at me, my loyalty is unwavering. I know he's trying to protect me the best way he knows how.

I choose the same approach with my mother, and as soon as I let go of my own righteousness, they both soften. *My own attachments to them changing their minds was actually fueling the fire.* Once I surrendered into What Is and just decided to keep my heart open while also increasing my discernment around what I do and do not share with them, the dynamics were able to harmonize again.

Truth is, I'm grateful.

Both my mom and Jay have illuminated aspects of myself that still needed approval and validation from others to feel secure in my choices. They've been good training for what is to come once we publish this book for the whole world to see, especially because their views will likely resonate with the vast majority of the population much more than our fringe perspective. And as much as I trust their triggers to teach me, I also trust that the triggers I activate in them can provide good medicine for their journeys, should they choose to see it that way.

The path of radical internal and external transformation is not for the faint of heart. It is often a lonely one, marked by opposing forces of skepticism, judgment, fear, and confusion. If we can learn to embrace those forces as teachers, guiding us ever closer to the Truest Truth within ourselves, we'll soon realize nothing and no one can deter us from B ≡ Ϙ O M I N Ϙ who we were always meant to be.

It is our birthright. If we just claim it.

WHAT ARE YOU WILLING TO RISK TO OWN YOUR TRUTH?

"If you think you're enlightened, go spend a week with your family."

—Ram Dass

We: Reality is, our human tensions, disappointments, heartbreaks, and misalignments actually make life rich, complex, and interesting. They keep us evolving. They provide traction. They give us the opportunity to see and understand more of ourselves in the reflection of others.

That doesn't mean we have to keep unconsciously re-creating the same painful patterns in relationships, though. Through the willingness to open our hearts again and again, we can collapse the power of unconscious patterns and transcend them altogether.

It is actually very common for those of us on the path of B ≡ Ϙ O M I N Ϙ to move through a phase in which there's pushback from our inner circle. Family dynamics can be especially challenging, because all of the undigested material from a life shared mostly unconsciously will surface to be transformed.

Why is the B Ξ Q O M I N G process often so triggering to those not on the path?

When one of us steps out of the status quo with the courage to self-actualize, our energy ripples out into the collective and sheds light on areas where untapped potential still resides. The people we love and care about can choose to see our courage as inspiration, but if they themselves have not addressed their own B Ξ Q O M I N G, it is likely that they will feel an uncomfortable or painful reflection. Most people will project that discomfort onto the "source" of the change or the disruption; blame, shame, anger, and avoidance are common manifestations of this projection. When we're triggered to look at ourselves more deeply and challenge what we've known, most of us tend to defend and protect ourselves—guarding the identities that we have become comfortable and safe in. It's a fascinating and often heartbreaking phenomena that we have seen occur in the lives of many of our clients and allies, as well as in our own lives.

Remember, the pottery must first break so that it may be put back together with gold. Our relationships are not exempt from this process of transmutation, but the ones that make it through this death/rebirth process are often the most beautiful ones yet.

Let's examine it more closely. We human beings tend to cluster together in social groups that have a predominantly shared worldview, or framework, of reality. Even if we don't agree on everything, there's generally going to be a pretty significant overlap in terms of preferences and aversions.

We call this *resonance*.

We are (mostly) on the same page with the five people we spend the most time with, and those five people in turn reaffirm and strengthen our worldview through their reflections. It is in this zone of homeostasis that we live out our lives until there's a pattern interrupt. That pattern interrupt can come in a variety of ways—sometimes it's a traumatic event like a sudden death, a serious illness/injury, the loss of a career, falling in love with someone distinctly "other" to the status quo, or—in some cases—a transformational and/or spiritual experience. In any case, we are talking about the kind of interruption that shatters the previously adopted lens on reality. In screenwriting, we would call this the "inciting incident." It's the moment in the script (usually within the first 10 pages) where the hero is jarred out of their comfort zone and forced to begin "the quest" of transformation because something out of the ordinary has kickstarted the story into motion.

You, reading this book, are the hero, and depending on how far down the path of B Ξ Q O M I N G you have already gone, you will know exactly what we are talking about.

What, then, happens to the inner circle when the hero suddenly breaks away from the rest of the herd and questions the consensus reality that has been shared (usually very unconsciously) up until that point?

Well, there's two options. Either the inner circle members can be inspired to accompany the hero on the quest of B Ξ Q O M I N G the hero of their own stories, and the subsequent shared adventure fuses them together even more closely, or they will reject the hero's quest and feel greater and greater dissonance as the gap between the old normal and the new normal widens.

This creates painful tension, and the emotional attachments we often cling to can interfere with the hero's quest to expand beyond the comfort zone of their known reality. If you have enough inner circle members who are also B Ξ Q O M I N G their own hero, you eventually end up with The Avengers, which is when life gets really fun. But that usually takes time.

First, you and those you love will inevitably get triggered, which is why the best option is to make triggers your best friend.

THE 5 T's: TRUST THE TRIGGERS TO TEACH

On her path of B Ξ Q O M I N G, Azrya has channeled and anchored in certain mnemonics that act almost like pieces of software coding in her consciousness. One of them is: The 5 T's: Trust the Triggers to Teach.

We've found that when sincerely integrated and applied in every-day situations, The 5 T's can become the ultimate cheat code to life. If you can master this mindset, you are well on your way to B Ξ Q O M I N G Unfuckwithable.

So, what is a "trigger" and how do you trust it to teach you?

A trigger is a psychological and emotional button that gets pressed and releases information in the form of thoughts and feelings. Like double-clicking on a zip file, when a trigger activates in your system, it expands and reveals something that previously existed but was hidden from sight.

Most commonly, a trigger is referred to as the surfacing of feelings on the shadow/fear side of the spectrum and implies that a disturbance has occurred within the internal landscape. Often, triggers are activated by external sources. Triggers can be as subtle as your spouse forgetting to take the trash out, which might trigger a feeling of not being appreciated or in some extreme cases could even trigger the feeling of not being worthy of love. The trash is not the issue. The deeper wound underneath the trash is the thing crying out for attention. Likely, the origin of that pain point has nothing to do with your spouse but stems from your childhood.

Sometimes triggers come in clusters, and when you've uncovered one, it leads you to a whole slew of others. This might sound awful, but it's actually a wonderful discovery! When this happens, congratulate yourself for hitting the jackpot. Once you've learned to embrace and diffuse those triggers like a very delicate bomb, great relief will come, for you've finally liberated yourself from that incessant internal ticking that you could never quite put your finger on.

Learning to identify your triggers is one of the greatest gifts you can give yourself and others. Eventually, you'll become an expert in navigating your triggers. In the beginning, you might notice that a lot of things trigger you. Annoyance and agitation are pretty normal sensations that most humans experience on a day-to-day if not moment-to-moment basis. But trust us when we say: There's a whole reality that exists beyond the triggers.

GIVING BIRTH TO OURSELVES

Almost all of us on the genuine path of B ☰ Q O M I N G will find ourselves, at some point, torn between the old and the new world. This is why the embracing of death is such a crucial component to this work. The caterpillar can never evolve into the butterfly if it is unwilling to give up being the caterpillar and let its previous form completely dissolve. The thing is, the caterpillar must be willing to do this without having any idea that it will become a butterfly. It will need to trust implicitly in the evolutionary pull of life's intelligence working through it to willingly face the chrysalis and go through such a rigorous initiation.

Humans are no different. We must learn to trust the unknown again and again as life initiates us into B ☰ Q O M I N G the Truest expressions of ourselves. The cost for that is our identity, which is mostly constructed out of false ideas of who we think we *should* be. The people in our lives who are deeply attached to our identity because it validates their own identity might kick and scream and try to convince us that we are making a mistake by trusting so deeply in something as vast, mysterious, and volatile as life. They might call it naive or even dangerous to believe in a benevolent and intelligent universe. Even changing basic things like reducing your consumption of animal products and alcohol can become a massive trigger for those around you who are resisting the change. We must remember that they likely have no tools with which to navigate their triggers and let them have their process. We must remember that they are fighting to preserve their framework of reality, and that we may become a perceived threat to everything they have chosen to believe. And we must take ownership for how we are co-creating the situation and look within at our own wounds that we may be unknowingly projecting outward.

This next visualization also helps us find more understanding for those who are triggered by our B≡QOMING.

Imagine you're an alien who just popped down onto planet Earth for some sightseeing and happened to land in a hospital room where a woman is in the middle of giving birth. The violent screaming, excruciating pain, blood, and mucus would create a pretty alarming scene, without context. But if you zoom out, you can—of course—see that birth is a beautiful thing, a natural thing, not something to cringe at or resist but something to celebrate (despite the blood, mucus, and occasional poop that comes with it).

On the journey of B≡QOMING, we are giving birth to ourselves. Sometimes, from the outside looking in, that can seem excruciating and destructive. But that's only because the context for the larger process isn't relatable yet. And trust us. The painful part of the birthing process won't last forever.

Compassion and discernment is key. If you are finding yourself triggered and therefore "reacting" versus "responding" to a naysayer's energy in a way that is creating more separation, sometimes the healthiest thing you can do is remove yourself, create some boundaries, and take space to process and integrate the emotions they are stirring up in you, for as the 5 T's guarantee, they will contain medicine for you to more deeply come into integrity within yourself.

Alternatively, if you can diffuse the trigger by taking ownership of it and genuinely respond rather than react, deeply listening and transparently sharing your perspective from a heartfelt, honest place can provide the healing balm of clarity and often dissolve separation.

In our experience, it tends to take many conversations and lots of time to allow a triggered loved one to truly understand the person you are B Ξ Q O M I N G. The trick is being fully committed and totally unattached to their process. If you genuinely want them to be a part of your new outlook on life, invest the time to make your process relatable and remember to *show* more than you *tell*. You can try and convince someone you're on the right path until you're blue in the face, but for most people, until they see the tangible results, it won't fully penetrate.

Those who are ready to walk with you will understand that in order for us to evolve, we must let go of who we have always been. If someone cannot let go of their clutch on what they think they know, or who they've decided you "should" be, let them fall away with grief and gratitude.

Not everyone is going to walk with us the whole way home.

INVITATION #6:

- What are your triggers, (i.e., what creates a visceral contraction or adverse reaction in your emotional state)?

- Pick one specific trigger, close your eyes, and evoke the feeling of it in your body. Observe the sensation, then – **ask to receive the gift contained within the feeling**. What comes up? What would it look like for you to respond to this trigger rather than react?

- Who in your inner circle is supporting your **BEQOMING**?

- Who is resisting your **BEQOMING**? What feelings / memories are they stirring up in you? How did you co-create the situation (i.e., where can you take responsibility)? Write them a letter. You don't necessarily have to give it to them.

- Using your discernment, decide whether you get to create healthy boundaries or lean in and support their understanding of your **BEQOMING**.

7

THE MEDICINE OF SEX

"If you have mastery over your physical body,
15–20 percent of your life and destiny will be
in your hands. If you have mastery over your
psychological process, 50–60 percent of your life
and destiny will be in your hands. If you have
mastery over your very life energies, 100 percent
of your life and destiny could be in your hands."

—Sadhguru

Bee: I'm 14 years old, and I've never gotten the sex-ed talk from my parents. My source of education (and inspiration!) has come solely from Victoria's Secret magazines and the JCPenney catalog bra section. Now I'm sitting in my friend's backyard at a party and a high school senior walks up to me with a glint in her eye. Next thing I know, she's lured me into a pitch-black tiki hut and we're making out, hard.

"Do you have a condom?" she asks, as she's about to unzip my pants.

I don't. In fact, I've never even seen a condom. But of course she can't know that. I tell her I don't have one on me.

"Go get one," she commands.

I scurry out of the tiki hut and find a girl who's willing to sell me a condom for $10. At this point, I would have paid anything. Victorious, I return to my steamy cheerleader, wrangle the condom from its packaging, and find myself inside of her. The next 20 seconds are the best of my entire life. Then it's over.

I'm in heaven, but my girl is just getting started. "Go get another condom," she tells me.

It's only now that I realize something terrible has happened. *The condom has evaporated!* I panic. In the darkness and with no clue how a condom actually works, I was unable to unroll it. I had just placed it on the tip, backward, and hoped for the best. Now I'm seeing my life flash before my eyes. *Ohmygodohmygod I just got her pregnant, my life is ruined!!!* Our tiki hut romance is over just as quickly as it started.

The anxiety persists until I'm lying on my friend's couch an hour later, and realize that *I am still wearing the condom!!!* Miraculously, it rolled itself down during the act. Elated, I decide God loves me and promptly pass out.

I don't remain clueless about condoms for long, and soon my sex drive eclipses any remnants of shame programming I'd picked up in my all-boys Catholic military school. Chasing women becomes an intrinsic part of who I am, and years later, after my divorce, I unleash the hedonist in me. My weekends revolve around blowing off steam, having fun, and chasing women. But I'm also never satisfied. The chase is just as gratifying as the reward, and I'm addicted to the high of having women give me their bodies, even if just for one night. I learn that unapologetic sexual energy is potent, and I use it to magnetize women into my field to generate a false sense of validation and power. I don't always use that power responsibly. After several years of playing "the game," it loses its appeal.

I crave depth. I want to build something real with someone, something lasting.

When I meet her, Azrya shatters any preconceived notions of what my "type" is. Her confidence, heightened sensitivity, and willingness to surrender to peak physical and emotional sensation is an incredible turn-on for me. It's not uncommon for her to shed post-orgasm tears of gratitude and awe as she allows her body to become a portal into the most transcendent states of heart-open bliss. For the first time, I feel like I can pour myself completely into a woman and be fully met, on every level.

My introduction to sex was about as unconscious and unintentional as it gets, and that pattern continued for most of my life. Azrya—and the B Ξ Q O M I N G process our love has catalyzed in me—has been the ultimate invitation to bring more presence and awareness to my sexuality. Through our union I am learning how to wield the true power contained within it and finally use it as a force for good.

Azrya: I am five years old and have somehow discovered that rubbing myself on the edge of my mother's piano bench unlocks the most ecstatic sensations of bliss that expand from between my legs all over my body, like being filled with warm honey.

But the sensation doesn't last long. My beloved babysitter walks in on me, and I can instantly feel she's alarmed. Without saying a word, she turns around and shuts the door. I don't know what I did wrong, but I know it was somehow connected to this feeling of ecstasy, and so I decide it's not safe to freely explore it any further.

From then on, my erotic innocence is repressed, shrouded in a memory of shame, and I feel increasingly inhibited and insecure in my skin. Puberty amplifies these feelings. I watch my peers begin to explore their sexuality, but it feels so out of reach to me. A giant wall of sheer terror stands between me and other bodies. I have chemistry with boys and even girls, and I long to express this part of myself, but the fear is debilitating. Sometimes I wonder if I will ever be able to overcome this.

At 17, I lose my virginity to my first boyfriend while we're in Paris. He's a tall, German-Russian classmate of mine, and he loves me. The experience is sweet, tender, and heartfelt, but the feeling of not being fully free to tap into the full expression of my pleasure stays with me all the way into my late 20s. At that time, I discover the modality of sexual healing. It's humbling to acknowledge that I require professional support to feel safe and free in my body.

The modality I choose teaches me that our body is essentially a living library of our subconscious mind, which stores information about our past experiences. Sexual healing entails releasing stored traumatic imprints from the body and the sexual organs through various hands-on techniques. Traumatic imprints can be extreme, like rape—or in my case, more subtle, such as shame imprints from childhood. Either way, these imprints cause disconnect within the body's ability to open to heightened sensations such as orgasm.

Like in a very intensely painful deep tissue massage, the trained practitioners I work with loosen up the stagnant energy of various old, traumatic sexual imprints I had collected and then help me pave over those physical and emotional pain points with pleasure.

There's this saying, "the issues are in the tissues." After seven three-hour long sessions of lying naked and blindfolded on a massage table in a darkened room while crying, sobbing, and screaming my way through the healing process, I learn to surrender into the intense sensations of both my agony as well as my ecstasy, and slowly build trust with my body again. This alchemical process creates a psychological rewiring in our limbic brain.

I learn that not all of the painful imprints that were lodged into the cells of my body are even "mine"—many are from the collective feminine pain body. The practitioners help me safely transmute these energies by supporting me to feel the suppressed emotion fully, once and for all. This allows me to reclaim my power from the past so I can use it in the present. It's emotional alchemy.

We can literally learn to transform pain into pleasure at will. We just have to be willing to feel all the things that no one wants to feel.

I had no idea that through this work, I was preparing my body to be able to meet Bee and experience the full-blown activation of my latent sexuality. As we enter the realms of sexual union, Bee not only gives me full permission to explore and expand the "wild one" in me and discover new levels of surrender, creativity, and play within the arena of sexuality—he demands that I hold nothing back and give myself completely to the potent force of our primal connection. With Bee as my trusted pillar, grounding all of my cosmic energy into the physical realm simply by being himself, I am finally safe to go beyond the edges of my comfort zone.

Which brings us back to Mars, and how it all began.

MARS

I have Benjamin to the right of me and Mars to the left of me, and I know that if this dinner is going to become more than a casual hang out, I'm going to have to be the one to initiate it. I play it cool on the outside, but on the inside I'm feeling like an amateur. *Oh my God, am I really about to make a move on my girl Mars?* We've known each other for a couple of years and established a solid friendship, which I am about to potentially put at risk by hitting on her. Truth is, I'm less concerned about being rejected and more concerned about making her feel awkward. But I respect and trust Mars to know herself and her boundaries, and so I decide it's time to put my cards on the table. This is an edge I've been tip-toeing around for too long, and I'm complete with letting fear and shame inhibit my ability to experience the richness of life. I decide transparency is the only strategy.

"I have a confession to make," I tell Mars over dessert, marveling at her natural beauty and caramel skin. "Bee and I are attracted to you, in case you couldn't tell." Mars smiles; she seems at ease and receptive.

"I'm honored," she replies, "and down to explore what that could mean."

A beautiful and honest conversation ensues, during which Mars asks us questions and I share about my lifelong attraction to women, and that I don't have a jealous bone in my body. It's my great reverence of the feminine that's underneath my desire to connect more intimately with her.

After dinner, we all head to a party, but none of us really want to be there, so we soon come home, light a few candles, and find ourselves on the couch. The energy is thick with potential, but I'm not sure what to do next. I can talk about anything, but this part is out of my wheelhouse.

"I'd love to see you two kiss," Benjamin suggests, calm as a cucumber. Of course, he effortlessly gives voice to the unspoken tension in the air. I decide to tuck a strand of Mars's thick, dark hair behind her ear and lean in close, feeling her breath on my skin. My heart rate speeds up. Then I go in for the kiss. Her lips are plump and infinitely soft. So different from kissing a man. I melt into her warmth. *Yummy. Earthy. Tender. Wise.* From that point forward, everything feels natural and easeful.

Mars initially sets the pace by joining us in the bedroom as a witness to our love, rather than an active participant. Her energy in the space contributes a beautiful dimension of sensation, like adding a drizzle of chocolate syrup to an already delicious cake. She is strong, intelligent, spiritually awake, and deeply connected to her body.

Is this really my life?

I feel so blessed and honored to experience such a powerful, beautiful woman in this intimate way. Sharing Bee with her just feels right. His pleasure is my pleasure. There is no separation for me.

Sometimes I can feel Bee bracing himself for a moment, wondering if I'll ever get jealous or insecure. But it never happens. Instead, the three of us develop a beautiful connection that is much more than physical. Mars joins us for hikes, meals, ceremonies, and deep conversations. There are long periods of time where she requests that our dynamic shifts to being purely platonic, and Bee and I both honor what feels true for her. Mars also gets to override some of her shame programming and, over time, gives herself permission to lean into this beautiful relationship with us.

Making love to Mars is magical. "Her feminine curves, insanely soft skin, and nurturing heart gives me deeper appreciation for my own femininity," I share with Bee in the bathtub one day. "It's like she acts as a mirror that allows me to fall more viscerally in love with my own body."

We are both genuinely falling in love with Mars, and that love is facilitating growth and expansion for each of us. The dynamic between the three of us is such a testament to what is possible when shame, judgment, and fear aren't steering the ship. On the other side of stripping away all the inherited stories around the "right" way for love to express itself, there is so much beauty and connection to be enjoyed. I am in awe of how effortless it all is.

Mars's energy isn't adding something that is missing. She's amplifying the goodness of what's already there. And it's only possible because I did the work to liberate myself from the shackles of shame and fear and finally came home to the innate intelligence and innocence of the most valuable gift I have ever been given by creation: *my body*.

BODY INTELLIGENCE

We: Imagine aliens pop into your living room, invite you onto their spaceship, and take you to their dimension for some sightseeing. They show you around, and proudly tell you about these very sophisticated creation machines they've developed. The machines are made of organic materials and complex energy circuits and act as vehicles that the aliens can operate with the "fuel" of their intentions.

The better they get at operating the vehicles, the more precisely they can imagineer which version of reality they want to experience. Almost like a "choose your own adventure" video game, these vehicles are capable of literally shaping and molding the fabric of reality through mastering a variety of vibrations and sensations.

You'd probably be pretty inspired to hear about this. You might even wish that there was such a thing on Earth.

Well, guess what. There is.

It's called *your body*. And you're the one in the driver's seat.

Because we live in a world that appears to be limited to the five senses, we generally don't think of the body as a multidimensional vehicle that our consciousness is inhabiting. We don't always have the awareness that our body consists of both physical as well as non-physical layers.

In our opinion, the human body is a living, breathing miracle of creation, and yet most of us relate to it like a caveman might to a MacBook Pro. He could figure out how to put it in the sun and fry an egg on it, which would be very advanced for him, but the truth is: he's never even found the Power On button. That Power On button is your turn-on. Your orgasmic, aroused, pleasured state quite literally turns you *on* to receiving the flow of life-force energy that inhabits all living things.

If we could give our bodies and the energetic currents running through and around them even a fraction of the same amount of interest and attention as we give our social media feeds, we'd be lightyears further ahead as a society than we are right now.

We're not talking about putting attention solely on your appearance. That is just the outer shell, the very first layer. We are talking about cultivating an intimate relationship with the ancient intelligence of your bones, of learning to listen to the whispers of your cells, of becoming attuned to the subtle energy fields that make up your aura, and of communicating with the dormant wisdom encoded into your very own DNA. Just in the way a lamp emits light, your body is constantly emitting a magnetic field of energy that is either contributing a positive charge to any given space or draining that space because it is, itself, depleted.

When it comes to this life, the body *is* the prize. The body is an incredible portal that can propel your consciousness into the depths of sensation, as well as the heights of the astral realms. It is not something to be "transcended," as many spiritual teachings would have you believe.

You can access the sophisticated capabilities of the body by inhabiting it fully, with every last little bit of your awareness. Just like a lover will open up and blossom if you adore every last inch of them, your body will respond similarly if you begin to devote yourself to understanding, caring for, and nourishing it. It's a profound shame that we were never taught how to truly relate to our bodies, for they carry so much wisdom—right under our noses.

The first step to rectify this is to find the right Q, the question that can then inform the action that is taken. For example, if the question is "Why do I feel uneasy in my body?" the intention can organically form to bring more awareness to food choices, suppressed trauma, or self-rejecting thought-patterns.

The question is always the entry point that will lead you to the next step on your unique journey of BΞQOMING. **A powerful, clear question magnetizes into itself opportunities to find answers.**

No two bodies are alike, which is why we cannot look for external, one-size-fits-all solutions. Our bodies literally force us to learn how to listen to them and honor their individual expressions. We cannot bypass the necessity to cultivate awareness within ourselves. All we can do is keep asking *why*.

The answers are hiding in plain sight. If you keep asking and listening, life will provide you with the next steps to take. If you trust life and actually take those steps, more steps will reveal themselves, and you are now officially participating in the BΞQOMING game.

SEXUAL INTEGRITY

"The difference between rape and ravishment is love."

—David Deida

Sex is a subject that affects all of us, and it might be the most confusing one yet. Everywhere we look, sex is being sold to us, yet the education about how to navigate this highly complex area is sorely lacking, and the maze of shame and trauma that distorts the subject is overwhelming to say the least.

Whether we are aware of it or not, most of us require some level of sexual healing. That work begins with illuminating the subject of sex within your own life and starting to dig deeper into your sexual history.

Whether you're gay, straight, pan, kinky, or "traditional" is less important than how you feel. Again, it's not so much about *what* you do, it's *why* you do it, so if your heart and spiritual channel is open enough to see the divine infused into matter, and both the giver and the receiver are in their Full Fuck Yes timeline, then the body becomes a temple, a shrine, an altar upon which to pour love, gratitude, and devotion.

Sex, then, becomes far more than a carnal act. It becomes a spiritual practice, which replenishes the mind, body, and spirit with an infusion of high vibrational life-force energy and allows us to become greater embodiments of our true radiance. Through the exchange of this energy and harnessing the power of pleasure, we can literally charge each other up like batteries, strengthening the electromagnetic field that emanates from every human body and making each other more alive and creative.

But it can also go the opposite way.

You've surely heard the saying "with great power comes great responsibility." If you think about it, sex is a very powerful act, if not the *most* powerful act. What else can generate the kind of creative energy that initiates something as delicate, meaningful, and complex as the creation of another human being? No man-made technology can do that. Only the vast intelligence of our bodies know how this works, and they do it over and over again.

Sadly, most of the time, the act of sex is performed very unconsciously. The immense creative power contained within the act is not revealed to us unless we actively start looking for it. When we do, we may uncover the ancient wisdom traditions that have practiced sacred sexuality for thousands of years and learned to harness sexual energy in many ways beyond the purposes of procreation.

In our modern culture, these esoteric practices have become lost to everyone except the devoted seeker. Today, many of them are resurfacing, albeit with a fair amount of misinterpretation and confusion around what they entail and how to appropriately apply them, as we see in the burgeoning tantra community. Harnessing sexual life force energy doesn't actually have to look anything like the narrow definition of sex our culture has adopted. Whether it be the art of semen retention or breathing practices designed to activate our vital life force without even needing to get undressed, there are many tools available to us that can serve the full activation and embodiment of our most creative expression on the path of B⹃QOMING.

The body is profoundly intelligent, and it will heal itself if we give it the opportunity to do so by creating the right conditions. Sex is the ultimate merging of bodies, so when we choose to perform this intimate act, it is incredibly important to remember the responsibility of sharing one's energy in such a literal way. We literally imprint ourselves upon another, so let's make sure we are in integrity with ourselves before we do so.

We believe that the body, and its innate capacity to experience delightful sensations of pleasure and connection, is too precious of a gift to keep shrouded in a veil of shame, confusion, and silence any longer. We invite you to dissolve the taboo and start getting really honest about how sex shows up in your life.

DESIRE

The Buddha teaches that desire is the root of all suffering, and yet desire is an innate component of the human condition. It is an evolutionary force that propels us to reach, grasp, and cling to fleeting sensations, whether they be comfort, food, sex, or power, usually keeping us at odds with the impermanence of our reality yet, at the same time, ensuring our continual growth as a species, for better or worse.

Eventually, we all must come face to face with our deepest desires, whether they be expressed or repressed, and understand our relationship to the raw material of desire itself.

In *The Gene Keys*, Richard Rudd describes the shadow of desire as "genetic hunger, a hunger for experience itself." This shadow compels us to expand in all directions of the spectrum until we have exhausted the notion that our desire will ever be fulfilled. It is precisely when we come to fully embrace, accept, and even celebrate the fact that we will always be destined to yearn and long as an intrinsic part of our human makeup that we can transform the power of desire and turn it into a gift. This requires "an inner surrender that cannot be forced or faked," as Richard describes it. It is when we finally throw our hands up and simply stop desiring to end our desire that we escape the suffering that comes from it. This then liberates us to dance with our desire, to witness, channel, and harness its intelligence and not be enslaved to it. Once again, it is not the thing itself that must change but rather our reaction to it. That is where all the power of our free will lies dormant.

It is actually quite hilarious to realize that even our desire to BΞQOMΞ the best version of ourselves is still, at its core, a desire—and can itself become a trap. The incessant desire to become better, more aware, more at peace, more enlightened can be the very thing that keeps us from embodying those exact traits. It's a paradox that our logical mind cannot escape, which is why the ultimate transmutation occurs through the power of humor. When we "give up" and simply learn to laugh at the mystery and often nonsensical nature of this human experiment we are all participating in, that is when we graduate to the next level where we can bask in our desires without being attached to them.

When we realize *there is always further to go and nowhere to get*, that is when we BΞQOMΞ free.

INVITATION #7:

- How at home in your body do you feel right now? Do you experience the joy of feeling fully nourished or the toxicity of neglect?

- When you look in the mirror naked, what are the immediate thoughts / feelings that arise about your body?

- What belief systems do you hold about pleasure? I associate sex with...

- I learned about sex from...

- Define what being in integrity with your sexuality means to you? Are you in integrity (based on your definition)?

- If not, what steps do you need to take to stabilize your sexual integrity?

- What is your relationship with desire? Where does it have power over you?

8

REPROGRAMMING YOUR OPERATING SYSTEM

"The problem is not that there are problems.
The problem is expecting otherwise and
thinking that having problems is a problem."

—Theodore Rubin

Bee: After the intensity and backlash of the surprise union ceremony has subsided a bit, we are both excited to turn our attention back to our mission, which includes designing the B Ξ Q O M I N G coaching process, filming a documentary, and writing this book.

But at the same time as Azrya begins extracting her key learnings from 35 of her jam-packed journals to start the creative process, I am hit with a barrage of lawyer bullshit. The lawsuit is now starting to rear its ugly head again as we ramp up for court hearings, and every month $100k–$200k is going toward legal fees alone.

The financial and emotional stress is sucking me dry energetically. The more excited I am about all the projects Azrya and I are
co-creating, the more being forced to deal with this mess is taking
a toll. *You made peace with the situation*, I try to convince myself.

It's partly true. I did release a lot of the anger and resentment toward
my opponents and genuinely feel deep gratitude for the fact that this
painful situation led me to birthing my Personal Operating System,
which has since evolved into the B Ξ Q O M I N G Operating System.
But a deep-seated frustration that I'm being robbed of valuable time
and resources I could be investing into actualizing my newfound
purpose still lingers. I feel painfully trapped by my past mistakes.

My sleep goes out the window. Every night, I'm up for several hours,
squinting at the blue light emitting from my computer screen in
the dark, emailing lawyers while cortisol pumps through my veins,
draining my adrenal glands. Every morning, Azrya comes down
the stairs wearing one of my T-shirts and no panties. But even her
warm, silky skin on my lap isn't enough to permanently remove the
dark cloud hanging over my head. I'm consumed.

"What would it look like for you to just walk away from all of it?"
she has the audacity to ask me one day.

"What do you mean?" I retort. "That's fucking ridiculous."

Azrya takes a beat. "Okay," she calmly responds. "If walking away
truly isn't an option, let's dive into this then. Are you open to
receiving my reflection?"

"Sure," I say, bracing myself. Her reflections can be like daggers.

"What's at the core of your emotional frustration right now?" she asks.

"I'm just pissed that this is dragging on. I feel like I've already integrated the lessons from it and now I just want it to be over," I reply.

"Well, there's the blind spot," she says. "You're in resistance to *What Is*. The fact that this lawsuit is still here means it still has curriculum for you; otherwise it would be resolved already. You don't get to pick and choose to believe the universe is a benevolent and intelligent teacher only when it suits you. You either believe it all the time, or you don't."

I'm annoyed, but she has a point. I've allowed victim consciousness to creep in, and it's making me feel like shit.

"If we firmly believe that life is a reflection of our internal state, then we must also accept that it is doing that 100 percent of the time." She reminds me. "So—if there's randomness and chaos externally, it is simply mirroring that same energy within, in order to give you the opportunity to step into greater choice. Chaos happens when awareness has not yet taken the steering wheel from the hands of the monkey mind, which is driven mostly by subconscious survival fears. All of which are in overdrive for you right now."

My conversation with Azrya invites me to truly examine the question: *What if all the seemingly "negative" things that happen to us are actually components of a highly intricate plan shaped and executed by our own subconscious, our higher self, and the universe?* To truly trust in that intelligence—even when we have no idea what the fuck is going on, or why things are happening the way they are—is the spiritual initiation into installing an entirely new operating system. It's what allows us to graduate from victim consciousness into creator consciousness.

It is the one choice that shapes all others. And it's a lot easier said than done.

We: Remember in *The Matrix* when Morpheus presents Neo with the red pill and the blue pill? In that famous scene, Neo is being asked to choose—with his own free will—which version of reality he wants to exist in.

The '90s blockbuster movie did a wonderful job of bringing the concept of "awakening" into our collective consciousness. It did this by showing us how a single choice can change the trajectory of someone's life forever. It also painted the world as a dark and dystopian place, so we have developed a slightly different expression of what those two choices entail.

In our version, the blue pill represents a random universe in which there is good luck and bad luck, and no matter who you are or how you show up, life is mostly unpredictable and often ruthless. The vast majority of human beings exist in this place. They are asleep in the "dream," unaware that there is so much more to existence. You could also say that they are in a state of victim consciousness that says: "I have no or little personal power, and things are happening to me outside my control, which makes my ego want to control life even more. I project blame and refuse to take responsibility for co-creating my reality."

Our red pill represents awakening to a highly intelligent universe in which things happen for a reason, and we are loved by an unseen force that guides us toward the embodiment of our greatest potential, should we choose to participate in our own evolution. This entails us claiming our creator consciousness, which says: "I understand control is an illusion, and by accepting that I am always co-creating my circumstances and learning to master my internal state, I liberate myself from the shackles of fear and design my life from the inside out."

Choosing the red pill is not a choice you will make once. It's a choice you must be willing to make over and over again, for the rest of your life.

WELCOME TO THE DIMENSION THAT EXISTS BEYOND PROBLEMS

Azrya: Consistently waking up to an empty bed and finding Benjamin in front of his computer with dark circles under his eyes is starting to get to me. I can feel him oscillate in the schizo-phrenic dance between his fear-based ego clutching for control, while the voice of his Truest Truth KNOWS: "It's all happening *for* me." At the same time, his intellectual mind is grappling between the KNOWING that he has the power to not let this affect him, while his biological fight-or-flight response is proving otherwise by pumping his system full of stress hormones.

For weeks, I watch him find spurts of surrender and peace with whatever outcome the universe might deliver, only for an email or incoming call from his lawyers to kickstart the loop of worry and doomsday calculations all over again. In short, he's in a sort of purgatory within himself, and it's taking a toll on both of us.

I remain firm in my reflection that his *relationship* to the situation is where all the power resides. At the same time, as the weeks drag by, I am slowly beginning to run out of patient optimism myself. My own desire, which is to have a lighthearted, present husband with whom I can playfully co-create our shared visions for the future, is beginning to drag me into the same frequency of "wishing it was over" that I feel in him. I observe in real time how this state of resisting *What Is* begins to extinguish my creative spark.

Fuck. I hate to admit it, but despite all my best efforts and personal development prowess, I am triggered. The heaviness is activating my own ego's fear programs around my brand-new husband's ability and willingness to opt out of the stress and plug into the truth of his power by remembering that joy is an inside job. I can see him trying so hard to keep his center and know that pushing him into surrender by expressing my own discontent with the situation is not helpful, so I finally stop trying to inject myself into his experience, step back, and listen to my own chorus of schizophrenic voices yapping away in my head.

- My **fear-based ego**—who gets off on drama—is yelling, *"Listen to me!!!* This is a systemic problem that's bigger than the lawsuit! Once this is resolved, his ego will inevitably manifest an infinite array of future problematic situations that need attention because he is a problem-solving machine, and he's deeply attached to that identity as his source of self-worth! You need to be careful that you don't sacrifice your freedom, lightness, and joy for the sake of this relationship! *You need to fix this!!!"*

- My **intellectual mind**—who loves finding solutions—is logically communicating, "Yes, this is a problem, but it can absolutely be solved! If we could get him to meditate more, or do breathwork, or inspire him to go on a hike instead of sitting in front of his computer all day—then it would be better. Then he'd see that he has the power to change this. How can we get him to see that? Let's find a new angle to get him to view things differently. Okay. Here's one. Ask him to imagine himself on his deathbed, reflecting on his life. How important is this in the grand scheme of things? Yes. That could be the solution!"

- My **spiritualized self**—whose metaphorical feet never touch the ground—is cooing, "It's all happening exactly as it should be, darling. This situation contains invaluable gems, if only you are willing to look for the lessons and embrace *What Is!* 🙏"

- And finally, the voice of my **Truest Truth**—the one that exists beyond all of the confusion and thrives off of self-responsibility pipes in—full force. "Yo. *Everyone shut the fuck up for a minute.* Notice how you want *him* to shift his internal state first, so *you* can feel better? You want him to stop letting it get to him, so why don't you stop projecting and stop letting it get to you?

His lawsuit isn't your problem.
His attitude isn't your problem.
YOU—my dear—are your only problem.

Stop outsourcing your happiness, stop focusing on how to fix him, and lead by example. It's time to practice what you preach.

Mic drop.

Of course. If I'm really in creator consciousness, then I know that his stress levels can only affect me to the degree that I allow them to, just like the lawsuit can only affect him to the degree that he allows it to.

Boom. I'm back in the Dimension That Exists Beyond Problems. All it takes to exist here is the radical willingness to accept that every problem—at its core—begins and ends with *me* and my relationship to it. In one fell swoop, I can no longer point the finger at anything external and blame it for—well—anything.

From this perspective, I see the gift in all of it again. This whole situation is an elaborate initiation exercise for everyone involved to have the opportunity to reach a higher state of consciousness (myself included). I let go of needing him to be or do anything other than whatever the fuck he arrives at on his own. I make peace with all of it.

A couple of hours later, Benjamin, who had finally torn himself away from the computer and gone to the beach, comes home, sand clinging to his bare toes.

"I figured it out," he says, his demeanor much lighter than it had been a few hours before.

"Oh yeah? Tell me," I reply, as I gracefully chew my salad with my mouth closed (a new skill he has taught me, and one that I have proudly integrated after much trial and error).

He shares his new game plan with me. It's simple. He feels clear.

"What shifted it for you?" I ask, when he's done.

"I thought about my father," he replies. "My father spent three years building his dream house and hated every second of the process. He died less than a year later. I asked myself, if I had a year to live, how would I handle the situation from that place?"

"What was the answer?" I ask.

"If I had a year to live, I would either settle or walk away. But there's no way I'd spend it fighting. That was the shift."

I smile. But of course.

"Beautiful," I say, grateful to have my husband back.

A simple way to remember all this is:

The fear-based ego sees problems.
The true voice communicates opportunities.
The intellectual mind is in service to whichever voice is louder.

As Victor Frankl says in *Man's Search for Meaning*:

> Everything can be taken from a man but one thing: the last of
> the human freedoms—to choose one's attitude in any given set
> of circumstances, to choose one's own way.

We would argue that the entire point of the human experience is
the gradual awakening to and harnessing of our capacity to choose
our own experience of reality, in every moment, anew.

It is our triggers that illuminate the way to liberation.

TO BEE OR NOT TO BE

Azrya: I am sitting on a small pillow on the sandy ground, my back
pressed up against a tall palm tree, the afternoon sun warming my
skin. My eyes are closed, and from the outside, it looks like nothing
is happening. But on the inside, there are vast galaxies expanding

my cells, making my spine fuse to the hard, rounded trunk against which I am leaning and dissolving all perceived separation between myself and the tree.

Thirty minutes prior, Benjamin and I each drank a cup of Ayahuasca at a boutique resort in the desert,[3] having been called to facilitate a private ceremony for ourselves with the blessing of one of our teachers, who has seen our sincere dedication to the shamanic path and trusts our experience and capacity to navigate the medicine on our own.

Because of COVID-19, the Mediterranean-inspired vacation destination is closed to the public, but we know the owner, so we have the whole place to ourselves. It is here that we've decided to journey with the medicine together, and now, just as I am beginning to feel my spirit detaching from my body in order to explore the non-physical dimensions and retrieve the valuable information available there, I hear Benjamin screaming my name.

The tone of his voice instantly reveals that something is wrong.

As fast as I can, I pull my consciousness out of the ethers, back into my physical body and stand up, my legs like overcooked spaghetti. "I'm coming!" I call, as I make my way up the small path to the bungalow in which Bee is journeying.

---

3   We do *not* recommend drinking Ayahuasca on your own without a
     trained facilitator and having consulted your doctor, ever.

I enter the small space to find my husband butt naked and on all fours next to the bed.

"What's going on?" I ask, confused at the sight.

"I need to poop and I can't stand up," he says.

Well, that's a new one.

Earlier that day during a workout, Benjamin threw his back out. Since then, he had been experiencing a fair amount of discomfort leading up to our ceremony, but it was manageable. Now he's in debilitating pain, immobilized. Considering all that, his demeanor is cheerful.

"It's no accident, what happened this morning," he says, as I help him to his feet. "The medicine is showing me that the pain is a teacher. It's forcing me to surrender by bringing me to my knees—*literally.*"

Both his hands on my shoulders, we make our way to the bathroom. I step outside to give him some privacy, but soon he's calling me back in. "I can't turn around to flush," he says. I do it for him. Before helping him up from the toilet seat, we look into each other's eyes and I see the sparkle of pure possibility in his pupils. "It's all a choice. There's a timeline where I stand up and choose to have no pain," he says. He is tasting the vast potential of pure creator consciousness, the kind that exists beyond all limitations and can suspend even the laws of nature.

He rises to his feet. The pain has dramatically decreased, but the lessons that came with it remain long after we officially close the ceremony. After a lifetime of relentless rushing, pushing, forcing, and incessant doing, Benjamin is at a breaking point where he has no choice but to remember how to simply *be*.

Bee: Some people learn a lesson and are able to integrate it immediately. Others, like myself, are a little denser. Historically, I have had to be hit over the head with a lesson over and over again before I'm willing to try a different way.

While the medicine catalyzes significant shifts within people at a DNA level, it doesn't do the work for us. Instead, it gives us a reference point, a lived experience of what is possible—and then it's up to us to find our way back there on our own.

I walked away from the ceremony in the desert KNOWING that I cannot continue moving at the pace I am used to and, at the same time, resisting the lesson because of how excited I am about my newfound path. It's hard to admit that I am throwing myself into my purposeful work with the same intensity and relentlessness that I used to build my first business. Even though it's coming from inspiration, it's still taking a toll on my entire system, and my back pain and continued insomnia is a very clear sign that my body is revolting.

As always, life is the ultimate spiritual teacher, and the consequences of not being able to ease off the gas pedal and simply stop are becoming increasingly hard to ignore. At the same time as this awareness is coming online, it's also informing the B Ξ Q O M I N G course curriculum Azrya and I are designing together, and soon we come up with a name for the condition: The Doing Disorder.

I feel like a recovering adrenaline junkie. There's never a time when I didn't go hard. Even when I wasn't working, I was partying like a professional. In addition to the extreme sports, I was pulling all-nighters in Vegas and Miami and in general turning the adrenaline dial to the max. *More more more. Bigger better faster. Let's go.*

Now the same pattern is showing up in my transformational work. I am driven to expand, heal, transform, be of service. To purge and release all the toxicity I've collected over a lifetime of never letting it be enough. Very subliminally, though, there's a thread of fear woven into my Doing even now. It's the same scarcity program that I've seen show up so many times in my relationship to finances, except this one is related to a different fear: the fear of running out of time.

Underneath that is the same "not enough" story that has haunted me since I was a 10-year-old kid, striking out on the Little League team, unable to read a book. Not trusting myself to be enough is manifesting as a lack of trust in the divine timing of my life.

And it's ready to be transformed, once and for all.

Sometimes it's the little things that anchor our intentions into reality the most honestly. I have always been a slave to my emails, allowing them to dictate how present I am at the dinner table and giving them way too much power over my emotional state. As a business owner, I had to be available at all times. If I fell behind,

I'd wake up to 200 unread emails at 4 a.m. the next day and experience extreme anxiety.

As a demonstrative act toward myself and the universe to liberate myself from that deeply ingrained habit of always being at everyone's beck and call, I sit down at my computer and start drafting the following email auto-response.

Hello,

I have always been the guy that kept his email inbox at zero and responded to everyone. I have decided to explore a more passive approach that allows me to focus on my new path.

As you may already know, there have been some major life transitions for me which have come in response to my intention to embody greater purpose and channel my energy and resources into my new philanthropic endeavor, *www.B Ξ Q O M I N G.me*. This chapter of my life requires focus and spending less time on screens, so I apologize if I am unable to respond to your email.

I am grateful for your understanding as I navigate this new chapter of my life, and I am grateful for this opportunity to be of service in a new way.

I look forward to connecting outside the "inbox."

In gratitude,
Benjamin Bequer

That feels good. I can stand behind that. Proud, and already a little anxious, I make it live. An hour later I take it down, unable to withstand the intense obligation to respond that is hardwired into me and afraid of being judged.

Then I put it back up. And take it back down. I do that several more times over the following weeks.

It's a showdown between me, myself, and I. A hilarious little power struggle between how I've always known myself to do and who I say I want to be. It might seem silly, but it's not. It's an act of defiance, of choosing to let a huge chunk of my identity die so that a new, more balanced version of me can rise from the ashes of my inbox purgatory.

It's an act of self-love.

THE DANCE BETWEEN TIME
AND TIMELESSNESS

Azrya: It's 6:45 a.m. My mouth still hot and slick from milking Benjamin's cock, I lay in his arms, my face buried deeply in his neck, our limbs entwined, our positions purposefully maximizing the surface area of skin-to-skin contact. He drifts into post-orgasm sleep as I—wide awake yet motionless—contemplate whether to officially start my day or stay melted into his temple of a body. To extract myself would feel like prying apart two powerful magnets, thus creating a ripple in the mirror-like pond of this moment, disturbing its pristine capacity to reflect the infinite sky within.

The intelligence of my physical vessel knows exactly what it wants, which is to stay anchored in the sensation of complete interconnectedness, while my mind starts asking, *Shouldn't we get up and be productive? There's so much to do.*

I witness these two aspects of myself dance between time and timelessness, and realize that every moment contains this push and pull between Doing and Being.

How often does Doing win out? In a culture that celebrates tangible, measurable results, that almost fanatically worships productivity, I would say Doing is firmly in the lead. And yet, isn't fully soaking up a moment like this—in which the profound healing pleasure exuding from the person you love most is available without distraction—the whole purpose of being alive in the first place? How can a checkmark on my To Do list ever come close to delivering the satisfaction that is present in this moment of Non-Doing, of pure Beingness?

As I consciously choose to surrender to this Being state, I allow myself to access the portal of timelessness, and as I do—as my mind rests into the simple miracle of listening intently to the gentle snores coming from my sleeping husband—the beginning of this section suddenly and spontaneously begins to write itself in my awareness.

The words appear like holograms, free from any tinge of trying. They simply are, birthing themselves from the void of this timeless moment and thus confirming the direct correlation between the two states of Doing and Being, how they directly interface with each other, and how one cannot thrive without the other.

What I mean by this is: I could have allowed my drive to be productive and get on with my day rouse me to my feet as soon as the impulse To Do kicked in, and would have found myself in front of my computer a solid 30 minutes earlier, ready to punch letters into the keyboard and accomplish something I've deemed more valuable than the stillness I had just sacrificed in exchange. Likely, sentences would have appeared on the screen, and over time, a book would even be written.

The question is not whether the urge to To Do, to be productive, is not effective in the game of "getting shit done;" it is. The question is: *Where does that which is being created originate from?*

Is it infused with the frequency of "trying"? Or is it inspired by the frequency of "trusting"? How often are our actions unconsciously imprinted with the energy of *trying to get somewhere other than Here, because I don't trust Here to be enough?*

It is profound to consider that every action we take comes from somewhere. The origin of its impulse is usually unconscious. Why did I eat that extra cookie? Why did I just check my email again? Why are we writing this book? What is truly the intention? To *prove* to the world that we can create and complete something meaningful (lack frequency), or to watch in effortless awe how the information streams from the overflow of our internal wholeness (abundance frequency)? The simple act of stopping and checking in to identify where the impulse To Do is coming from can become the difference between a life worth living and a life that has passed us by.

Remember, the mind never gets tired of this common fairy tale: *Once I make it through my To Do list, then I'll be able to unwind and enjoy the moment.*

In theory, yes. In practice, the minute one To Do list is checked off, the mind instantly manifests a slew of new tasks to put in its place, because what's missing at the core is the ability to simply *be*. We are so very afraid of the Beingness, because there's nothing to hold onto. This is why Being and Trusting are so intertwined.

To trust the void—the silence between thoughts, the spaces between words, the microscopic pauses between breaths—is to trust beyond the confines of the mind, which clings to the world of the tangible. This trust deepens as the ego learns to shed layers of protection against everything it does not understand logically and cannot label and categorize within its existing map of reality. As the trust deepens, so does the access to new dimensions of creativity, insight, and revelation, until eventually, our day-to-day reality begins to illuminate moments like the one we began this chapter with, in which the portal to timelessness opens itself in a spontaneous act of grace, encoded with the invitation to surrender and receive the inspiration available there.

If productivity springs forth from this place, To Do lists become rich and nourishing rather than depleting and annoying. This is when the Doing Disorder turns into Devotional Doing.

It is from this place that Benjamin and I launch our B Ξ Q O M I N G Process beta group.

THE EGO AND THE MIND WALK INTO
A BAR AND FIND AWARENESS

We: The mind is an information processing machine; it diligently analyzes probable timelines and crunches data, scanning the known terrain of reality for problems to solve according to the ego's instructions, which demands that it prioritize perceived threats to our survival and the survival of the people and things we are most attached to. The ego can perform this threat assessment only by making a distinction between "us" and "them," "me" and "everything else." Therefore, the ego must separate us from Source, Spirit, or God (choose whatever term most resonates for you).

Just like certain baking recipes call for separating the egg from the yolk, "separation" in and of itself is not a bad thing. The ego, our "separate self," is a valuable part of our experience that gives us individuality. But you don't need to have a deep understanding of quantum mechanisms to understand that separation is actually an illusion, albeit a very convincing one, and when we become identified with our ego, we begin to generate a slew of problems for the mind to solve. The ego loves creating laundry lists of worrisome to-dos to calculate, rationalize, and strategize through. No wonder we are so exhausted as a species.

This dynamic between ego and mind is like a codependent relationship. They've got a good thing going—or so the mind thinks. But here's the key distinction: The ego can only continue to exist as long as separation is perceived as "real" and there are problems to solve. In order for there to be problems to solve, new problems must be generated.

In other words, the ego keeps the mind really fucking busy at all times, which gives the mind a purpose and our identities (which are usually indistinguishably entangled with the ego and the mind) a tangible source of fulfillment and accomplishment. The reward and relief that comes from solving a problem creates a momentary sense of satisfaction, which in turn, justifies the continued focus on finding problems to solve. This dynamic often leads to compulsive Doing.

When in this loop, the mind is so busy adhering to the ego's concerns, it doesn't have much time to be utilizing its tremendous creative potential beyond the world of perceived problems. It thinks it's being used in the best way possible, when in reality it's barely scratching the surface of its true purpose—which is to joyfully co-create our Full Fuck Yes timeline! The ego knows that if the mind discovers its true purpose it would get bored of solving fabricated problems and move on, so it does a pretty damn good job of convincing the mind that it is needed.

A great way to tell if your ego is at the helm is if things feel really fucking serious. Seriousness is the ego's alarm system, warning us of all the threats in the world we need to be protected from. But when we can give a breath to our seriousness, and gaze upon our life circumstances—no matter how challenging—through the gentle eyes of lightheartedness, we develop the ability to see things from our soul's perspective.

We are privileged to have the choice to integrate and use the ego in a healthy way, and we do this by deepening our awareness.

Awareness allows us to witness everything *as it is*. It has no opinion. It places no meaning upon the events it perceives. It exists beyond any semblance of separation. It is the infinite oneness, the Eye of Horus, the unwavering I AM presence. From the human perspective, looking at life through this lens of divine neutrality is how most mystics would define enlightenment. It's a lens that can be both deeply relieving as well as—eventually—a little bland.

When the ego is liberated from fear, that is when it starts to really deliver the gifts that come from our ability to perceive ourselves as separate, individuated, unique. If we're just part of the cosmic mush of infinite oneness, there's no hero's journey. There's no story, no drama to live out and mature from.

A dear friend of ours, Blu, once sat with Ayahuasca. During the ceremony, her ego walked into the room and had a conversation with her.

Blu asked, "What am I supposed to do with you?"

Her ego said, "Well, you have three options. Your first option is you can deny, judge, and repress me, which will just create an internal conflict. The second option is you can get lost in me—by putting me on and never taking me off. And the third option is you can dance with me—put me on in a useful way when you're telling your story, when you're performing, when you're sharing your gifts."

Blu was like, "Cool. I'll take option three."

It's through the integration of the ego, dancing with it, knowing when to put it on and when to take it off that we can start to enjoy the benefits of it. But like wearing a bra to bed, we must be able to take off the ego, lest we wake up in the middle of the night with it poking our sides.

Our problem-obsessed ego would like us to believe that it is a burden to have to continually examine and assign meaning to our reality—but this process is actually a tremendous privilege and opportunity to develop and refine the connection to the KNOWING of our Truest Truth.

PROGRAMMING THE SUPERCOMPUTER OF YOU

> "Your mind is like a knife that has cut into a cake. When you pull the knife out, it still has cake on it. Similarly, your mind retains the residue of many different past impressions and experiences. All these past experiences are stuck to your mind like cake sticks to a knife."
>
> —Sadhguru

In the airplane bathroom of a Delta flight, a small red sign reads:

GOOD HAND WASHING TAKES 20 SECONDS.
Or the time it takes to sing *Happy Birthday* twice.

As you lather your hands and read the sign, you might smirk at the clever choice of language. But would you ever stop to wonder *why* these instructions work? They can only work, after all, *because everyone knows the song.*

The real question is: *why* does everyone know the *Happy Birthday* song? Do you ever ask yourself where that song originated, or how the melody became an internationally recognized tune? You probably don't even remember when you learned it for the first time. (That's cool. Neither do we.) The point is, the song is such a normal component of your accepted reality that you never stop to question anything about it. It just *is.*

The same is true for so many aspects of your reality. And unlike the innocent *Happy Birthday* song, not all of those aspects are serving your highest good.

Take a moment to think of your body as a highly sophisticated quantum computer. In order for the system to function properly, you require both hardware and software.

- Your DNA, nervous system, organs, neuro-chemistry, etc., are the hardware.

- Your belief systems, thoughts, and frameworks of reality make up your operating system, which acts as the filter through which you interface with reality.

That operating system then has various "programs" installed into it that act as the software. These programs are the result of the parental and cultural conditioning you and your immediate circle are exposed to, and once they become hardwired into your system, consciously uninstalling or overwriting them with "software updates" doesn't just happen overnight.

First, it requires us to take inventory of what else we've blindly accepted as normal and included in our framework of reality with as little awareness as the *Happy Birthday* song.

This is why devotion is such a key ingredient, because the journey of B Ξ Q O M I N G requires not just significant software updates but also the removal of extensive malware and, eventually, the shift to an entirely new operating system.

Our most formative years are from ages zero to seven, a time where our experiences imprint us with what will become a large portion of our subconscious mind and form the cognitive foundation for the rest of our lives. Because so many of these imprints are shrouded in our subconscious, we must increase our bandwidth of awareness to pull them up from the databases of our memory and reexamine whether we choose to keep them running in the background or not.

We must also become aware (often painfully) how programmed and conditioned we are by the large-scale corporations who have entire fleets of marketing and advertising machines constantly devising new strategies for how to imprint themselves upon our psyche in a way that will most motivate us to consume their products. Do you know why you gravitate toward one brand of toilet paper over another? Why you focus on your body's imperfections rather than celebrating its natural beauty? Why you just checked your emails *again* even though you just decided to put the phone down 30 seconds ago?

Part of what makes being human today so complex is the mind-boggling amount of highly addictive, contradicting information we are bombarded with from every angle, all day, every day. Whether it's politics or nutrition, our social media feeds, or news outlets, the age of information has done one thing extremely well: confused, overwhelmed, and disillusioned us to the point where we have no choice but to start blocking out all the noise and go within to find our own Truest Truth. This is a gift, and in order to receive its medicine, we must be willing to shine the light of our awareness into the areas of our own psyche in which there isn't any.

We must learn to navigate the murky terrain of our subconscious.

We must embrace the shadow.

INVITATION #8:

- Pick a "problem" you are currently facing. How are you co-creating the situation? Explore what it would look like for you to take full responsibility for the situation, and note any perspective shifts.

- How "spacious" does your daily schedule feel? Is every minute of the day accounted for? Are you constantly Doing?

- What Doing tasks are the most challenging for you, and why? What's the internal dialogue around them?

- What Doing tasks are the most effortless, and why? What's your internal dialogue around them?

- Explore: How can your Doing become more Devotional?

PART 3

DIE BEFORE YOU DIE

9

ON THE OTHER SIDE OF DEATH IS ALWAYS TRUTH

"This is the shamanic dance in the
waterfall. This is how magic is done.
By hurling yourself into the abyss and
discovering it's a feather bed."

—Terence McKenna

Bee: The six-month coaching process Azrya and I designed has officially launched. We have an intimate group of clients (whom we call "allies") enrolled, and I am finding myself in the role of both teacher and student. I am a teacher in the classroom setting, walking everyone through the building of their own personalized Operating System. At the same time, I am still very much a student when it comes to the plant medicine ceremonies we have integrated into the curriculum.

You could say the BƎQOMING Operating System is the masculine container of Doing that grounds the feminine flow of Being, which the plant teachers facilitate, into form. And when it comes to Being, I still have a long way to go.

It has become our tradition to end each ceremony with a bath. Sitting in the soapy water across from Azrya around 3 a.m. after taking our beta-group of allies on an incredible journey with Ayahuasca, I decide to share what's on my heart.

"You know how we said we didn't need the legal paperwork when we married ourselves?" I ask. "Well, tonight the medicine allowed me to see that there was an element of fear in that for me. The part of me that didn't fully trust this love to last was hiding behind the fuck-the-system attitude. The truth is, I do want to marry you. Legally. I don't want there to be any holding back, any playing it safe. What's mine is yours. What do you say?"

Azrya's eyes widen. She takes a deep breath, then smiles. "Let's do it," she says.

Each of the retreats we host leaves me buzzing. This is the most fulfilled I've ever been. "It feels so good to pour myself into each and every one of you," I tell the allies during my post-ceremony share as I choke up, tears in my eyes.

Then the final retreat comes. The medicine hits hard and launches the space into a heavy process. Ayahuasca is like that. Unpredictable. Sometimes she feels like the sweetest nectar cooing us into higher realms; other times she slam-dunks us straight into the bowels of human suffering.

As I look over at Azrya throughout the night, she looks like she's frozen in time. Sitting upright on her mat next to mine, she doesn't move a muscle for hours. Her demeanor is serious. I can't read what's going on. She feels energetically distant, like she's a million miles away.

The next morning, Azrya's share in the integration circle is short and vague. "Last night was the kind of night that made me question everything I think I know," she says. I decide not to pry. She obviously needs time to process.

Azrya: My intention for this final retreat ceremony is: *to release anything blocking me from being a pure vessel of devotion.* I'm not sure exactly what I need to release, but I can sense there's something there.

Then the medicine hits.

I sit motionless on my mat as fear grips my spinal cord, pumping itself into my nervous system like chilled liquid lead. I don't know what's happening, but it feels like the medicine is confronting me with my worst nightmare: the fear of losing Benjamin.

Normally, even when I journey into the shadow territory of my subconscious, I understand the reason for it. The medicine's intelligent presence illuminates the lessons, even amidst the pain. The opportunity to transmute the suffering back into love through the full embracing of the pain is not always easy, but available, and by the time the ceremony ends I'm usually able to get there and come out on the other side clearer, lighter, and open-hearted.

But not this time. This time it feels like I'm looping in a dead end. Like I've just been delivered a death sentence and am being told I have no choice but to accept it. It feels like the medicine is showing me inevitable heartbreak is headed our way.

"There's nothing you can do," I hear, over and over again inside my head. "You will destroy him. It's already decided. Accept What Is." I can't even begin to know what to do with this information. I feel powerless, riddled with a feeling of guilt and betrayal. Close to midnight, I step outside by myself and sit in a moonlit chair overlooking the canyon. I am white as a ghost.

My mind tries to logically understand what this is supposed to mean. Benjamin and I have just started our lives together. We have thrown all caution to the wind, given ourselves fully to this union and our mission, and have repeatedly been shown that our love is medicine for the world. Why would Ayahuasca—our most trusted guide—pull the rug out from under us now? It doesn't make any sense. There is something deeper going on.

I can't put into words what I've been shown; I need time to process it on my own before sharing with Benjamin. With how much he's still processing his own emotional material and how seriously he takes the intelligence of the medicine, I know that sharing my doubt and confusion about our shared future while it's still so murky will only create havoc in him. I want to *will* the experience away, to just focus on the beauty and magic of my life, but the voice of my Truest Truth within urges me to do exactly the opposite. So instead of trying to run away from the fear that I've been shown, I decide to face it head on instead. Over the coming weeks, I sit with the hardest questions I can ask: *Is it possible that we aren't meant to be together for a lifetime? What could really threaten this love?*

The answer spontaneously becomes obvious: a child. Since Benjamin is a clear NO to having more children, the timeline in which I am a mother would require me being with someone else. The idea of that makes me feel sick to my stomach. Through deep reflection, meditation, and journaling, I start to recognize that the agony I was plunged into so viscerally during the ceremony is the same agony I felt as a 10-year old girl, when I was faced with the impossible choice between going to New York with my mother or staying in Germany with my grandmother. I realize I never processed that trauma, and now, here I am again, perfectly set up to recreate that same, no-win situation. The medicine never shows you something that isn't already within, even if it's completely hidden from view.

I don't yet know for sure that I am meant to have a child, but as I tune more deeply into my feelings, I see that the possibility is a crack in the foundation of everything we are building. What the medicine is illuminating is that if that crack is not addressed, it will grow over time and threaten the very fabric of our shared reality from the ground up.

Having a child is an act of devotion to forces greater than oneself, I write in my journal as I process. *Benjamin's unwillingness to even entertain the conversation is blocking life's intelligence to work through us.*

Even amidst all the confusion, I am certain about one thing: Should I wake up one day with the KNOWING that a soul wants to come through, it cannot happen with someone who does not feel the Full Fuck Yes to that child, and currently I can't see any avenue in which Benjamin will organically get there. I am terrified of having to choose between being in devotion to him and being in devotion to myself and Spirit.

I also realize that because I have been the catalyst for Benjamin to live his purpose, there's a tremendous amount of pressure that has accumulated toward not letting him down. Just in the way my grandmother had nothing to live for when I left, I can feel the part of me that is projecting that same, traumatic imprint onto Benjamin. I face off with difficult questions alive within me: *Do we need each other to live our purpose, our dharma? If, God forbid, I did wake up one day with the KNOWING that it was time to be a mother, would everything we poured ourselves into just crumble? Should the winds of time indeed pull us apart, would we see everything we've lived through together, all the unforgettable moments of pure bliss, creation, vision, and magic, through a prism of regret?* The idea of this being our fate is devastating.

Eventually, I can't keep it inside any longer. I have to share what's coming up with Benjamin.

In the first conversation we have about it, I am hysterically bawling my eyes out while Benjamin is calm and collected. He assures me that he's in the trust that whatever will happen, it will be right. But I can tell the reality of what I'm expressing hasn't hit him yet, not with the gravity it's hit me. It's still conceptual for him, just like it was for me until the medicine smacked me across the face with it.

Then the conversation about getting legally married comes up again. This time, the topic is accompanied by a sincere heaviness I cannot pretend away. I feel so torn. On the one hand, officially becoming Mrs. Bequer is all I want. On the other hand, I'm terrified of admitting that I am not able to make that promise with the uncertainty that is present in my body. Sharing my hesitation with Benjamin is the hardest thing I've ever had to do. It feels like a betrayal. But it's what's true, and I can't hide it any longer.

Thus the death portal begins.

DYING IN PARADISE

Bee: At the beginning of each year and as part of my B Ξ Q O M I N G Operating System, I set an overarching intention for the next 12 months. My theme for this year is being *fully committed and totally unattached*, a phrase that our friend and celebrity coach Peter Crone uses and one that deeply resonates with me, as I've notoriously become very attached to people and things and then suffered greatly when they didn't align with my expectations. It's important to clarify that I'm talking about a fear-based attachment here, not the healthy interdependence that forms between people who love each other.

Over and over again, the universe tests my ability to practice non-attachment. Whether it's related to settling the lawsuit, the conflicting opinions of others, or transitioning the dynamic with our beloved Mars into friendship after she shares with us that she's going to get back together with her ex-boyfriend—the theme is always the same: *Let go and accept What Is.*

But when I realize that Azrya is having real resistance toward getting legally married, the true impact of her process begins to hit me like a slow-moving freight train, painfully revealing just how deeply attached to this woman·I have become.

In my usual pattern, I find myself quickly going into a tailspin of worst-case scenarios. The child conversation had been a hypothetical possibility we discussed at the very beginning, and one that I swept under the rug because I didn't want to acknowledge it. But now it's staring me straight in the face, and with it, the realization just how entangled we truly are. Every aspect of my life has Azrya right smack in the middle of it, be it my purpose, my home, my family, or my community. Our long-term union being threatened feels like the very lifeblood of my reality is in jeopardy.

For the first time since we met, I don't want to be in the same room as Azrya. Her energy triggers a grief in me that is so deep, I don't know what to do with myself. The idea of us not being together feels like the greatest punishment I could ever receive from the universe, which is in direct conflict with the part of me that knows that **every perceived "problem" is just an opportunity waiting to be revealed, a gift wrapped in thorns.** All of the lessons we are integrating into our curriculum seem like a joke. *Trust the triggers to teach...yeah whatever—not this trigger! FUCK THIS TRIGGER!*

I am feeling about as far away from deep trust in the benevolence of life as I can right now. I've been committed to embodying the KNOWING that everything is happening *for* me, whether it appears that way or not. Yet, no matter how hard I try to see the beauty in this situation, I just can't get there.

Totally disoriented and seeking an escape, Azrya and I decide to fly to Tulum in the hopes that going back to the place we fell in love will help us see clearly. Being here again is surreal. The sun is still bright, the sky still indigo blue, the ocean still turquoise, and yet none of it is beautiful anymore. Memories of our fairy tale early romance haunt us at every corner. I immediately regret coming here.

"It feels like something is dying," I tell Azrya. "And I don't know what will be left on the other side."

Is the searing sensation inside of my chest demanding that I let go of the woman who I believe with every molecule of my being is the soul mate I've been searching for my entire life? I genuinely can't tell if it's the relationship that's dying or my attachments to it. The whole thing feels like a cruel joke.

Finally, I ask Azrya to give me some kind of certainty around whether or not she thinks having a child is inevitable for her. The limbo is killing me, and all of our long-term plans are on the line. Azrya goes to the beach to meditate alone and see if she can find clarity. She doesn't come back until midnight. I am wide awake and restless, genuinely wondering if throwing myself into this shared timeline with Azrya is the worst mistake I've ever made.

"I couldn't get a clear read," she says to me once she returns, as we lay in the dark on opposite sides of the bed, staring at the ceiling. "But if I had to pick between it being a possibility and it being a probability, I would say that the most honest answer is, it's a probability."

It's like my insides are being pulled out of me in slow motion.

If Azrya was like any other woman I've ever been with, I would be far less distraught about the situation because the women I've been with have historically always bent over backward to fit my will. But Azrya is a person who will never compromise her truth, even if it means losing everything. It is one of the things I respect most about her, and it is also the thing that terrifies me. She is a willing vessel for life's intelligence to work through her, and nothing—not even me—can get in the way of that.

Compromising my own truth is also not an option. I know with every cell in my being that if I were to agree to reverse my vasectomy and try to have a child from the fear of losing Azrya, it would be the wrong energy with which to bring life into this world. The fear would infect the entire process at a seed level, and ultimately, it would be out of integrity with the core of who I am. No matter which way I turn it, it's just not an option.

Really, the only options that remain are either to end it now, because the risk that we are fundamentally misaligned is too great, or release my attachments to this relationship lasting a lifetime and trust that whatever happens, every minute I get to spend with Azrya is worth whatever heartbreak the future might hold.

Azrya: Our time in Tulum is beyond intense. Endless conversations about why this is happening ensue. At times, it feels like this entire process is an act of divine orchestration, and I find myself tapping into an incredibly calm state of KNOWING that this is just another opportunity to surrender and trust more deeply than we ever have. Then the fear kicks in, and I spiral into guilt and despair, convinced I'm fucking up the most precious thing the universe has ever gifted me. My entire physical reality is fueled by the love that Benjamin and I share. It's the glue that holds it all together. I am not ready to watch it all dissolve before it's even really begun.

The medicine foreshadowed that I would destroy him. It feels like that's exactly what I'm doing.

On the fifth day, Benjamin finds me outside by myself at sunrise, staring over the water, truly contemplating whether it's fair to ask this man that I love with every ounce of my being to stay by my side without being able to deliver him any guarantees beyond tomorrow. Am I just making it worse? Perhaps the loving choice is to set him free, so he can find a woman who can give him the certainty he deserves. As I share these contemplations with him, my heart feels like it's being carved from my chest with broken glass.

He listens quietly, taking it all in and exuding a calm clarity that I have not felt in him before. "I woke up this morning to the realization that—no matter how much my ego wants to control the situation to feel safe—my heart cannot close to you. Not now, not ever. You are the greatest gift I've ever received. I'd be a fool to let you go. Whether we are together for a lifetime, a year, or a day, I surrender to What Is. And right now What Is, is that I adore you."

Tears flow from my eyes. *All I want is him.*

He wraps me in his big, warm arms and kisses me deeply. It feels like a million pounds have been lifted off of my shoulders—at least, for now.

THE BREATH OF FREEDOM IN
THE DEPTH OF COMMITMENT

Hearts, bodies, and minds intertwined once more, we leave Tulum in agreement that legal marriage is off the table and committed to choosing each other one day at a time. For as long as it feels true.

Then, a few weeks later, Benjamin decides to take a day off and focus on self-care while I'm out of town for the night. When I come home it turns out that he's pulled a 180.

"It's crazy," he says. "I had a vision where I viscerally felt the energy of a baby boy and suddenly had this KNOWING: If a child wanted to come through us from a genuine place of love, it would be the right thing."

I am amazed and elated. I, too, have been feeling the child—even received a name for him—but hadn't wanted to admit it. What had been a Full Fuck No has suddenly, almost miraculously, shifted. So everything should be fine now, right? Cue the wedding bells?

Not so quick. It soon becomes evident: There's more fear for me to process here.

Truth is a funny thing. It has many layers and faces. As I dig deeper and deeper into myself I find that while it is true that the child topic occupied a huge chunk of the fear and resistance toward marriage, there's a Truer Truth lurking underneath. One that I am having a hard time truly owning: *the fear of sacrificing my freedom. The fear of giving myself to someone, completely. The fear of losing myself. The fear of making a promise and breaking it.*

Once Benjamin opens the door to having a child, I can no longer escape this part of me who is terrified of making a lifelong commitment. I am ashamed of admitting that she's still in there, for it feels like yet another betrayal to the profundity of this love. All attempts to subconsciously suppress her have failed, as they always do when you are committed to living in transparent devotion to truth. She's asking to be witnessed, understood, and felt. So I finally do, and I start by asking *why*.

Why reveals that I really have no reference points for lasting marriages that are healthy, passionate, and truly vibrant, in fact, quite the opposite. I didn't see my mother in a committed relationship until I was 18, and I've never seen my absent father in one. Neither of them have ever been married. My grandmother was a widow by the time I was three years old. The vast majority of marriages

I've seen have been stale and tinged with resentment or well over-
due for a divorce. So it's not all too surprising that I have yet to be
deeply inspired by the institution of marriage.

I was a Full Fuck Yes to the surprise union ceremony because it felt
true to claim the power of this love on our own terms—with no
one except ourselves presiding over the ceremony. But something
about signing a contract and making it official has always felt stifling and presumptuous to me. This part of me questions: *Who are
we to know that this is meant to last a lifetime?* Nothing else in my life so
far ever has. My human experience has been marked by only one
constant: *change*. Change is the very nature of existence itself. How
can a promise that exists beyond the now co-exist with that awareness? If we really trusted the present moment completely, why
would we need any guarantees for the future? If love were truly
liberated, why should we bind ourselves to one person for life?

When I give this part of me a voice, I start to see that she has valued her own personal freedom above all else. She's fought for freedom, has been ready to die for freedom. The only commitment
she knows and trusts beyond a shred of doubt is her commitment
to her own personal truth and hard-earned independence. Her
desire to be light as a feather riding on the gusts of wind is out-
matched only by her desire to be taken, chosen, and claimed by
the masculine force of unwavering conviction. She wants to be
completely self-sufficient and simultaneously completely provided for. She lives and breathes paradoxes. Yes, it's the ultimate
mind fuck, and I didn't say that it makes any rational sense. She
wants both, she wants it all, and sometimes it feels like she refuses

to choose either fully, because if she did, the unknown would become the known, and the known is too safe, too predictable to keep her attention.

At a deeper level, she simply does not trust love to last. Her independence has become her shield, and it's guarding the very heart she so yearns to give to Benjamin as an act of devotion.

On the other side of those conflicting energies, the Truest Truth within whispers: *This way of being is not the end of the road. There's another layer deeper to go.* It's talking about a layer that I began to catch glimpses of when Benjamin and I read *The Second Mountain* together, in which author David Brooks writes:

> We live in a culture of hyper individualism. Over the past sixty years we have swung too far toward the self. The only way out is to rebalance, to build a culture that steers people toward relation, community and commitment—the things we deeply yearn for.

Benjamin's love has illuminated that yearning within me, and it feels foreign and scary and in direct contradiction with my entire previous operating system.

I decide to revisit the book, pulling it off the shelf at 1 a.m. one sleepless night and skipping to the chapters on marriage and commitment. *"You can't worship love and individuality in the same breath,"* I read. Damn. That feels uncomfortably true. *"Are you ready to lose control and be overwhelmed by marriage—come what may?"*

The hard truth in this moment is that no, *I am not fully ready.* Something within me is still resisting this initiation, and it isn't conscious. Rather, it feels very unconscious and hard to grasp.

Reflecting on my relationship with Adam, I see that even though we were together for almost a decade and certainly appeared incredibly committed, neither of us ever made a promise to each other beyond the present moment, so in a way it stayed safe for both of us. Even though we loved each other deeply and had the kind of connection people admired, when we bought furniture at Ikea, we still did it with a possible future break-up in mind. "I'll pay for the couch and you pay for the bed, so we'll know who owns what, if that day ever comes" he'd say. While the romantic in me cringed, the one who believed having an out is safer agreed.

Then came Benjamin, who claimed me for life. Except I haven't surrendered to him completely. I am still resisting the full merge. Threads of attachment to my identity of the independent woman remain intact, for she has served me well.

A couple months after Benjamin and I met, we got a reading of our astrology charts and how they interface with each other. I knew my friend and ally Zahara would blow him away with her approach. She practices what is called evolutionary astrology, which is not fatal-istic but rather free-will based. It shows you the energetic possibil-ities that the stars and planets offer you in this lifetime, and then you can choose how those energies manifest themselves in your reality. During the reading, Zahara said, "Your entire relationship dynamic can be summarized in one sentence: *finding the breath of freedom in the depth of commitment."*

She nailed it.

So how to find the breath in those moments where fear grips my throat? I remember the Fritz Perl quote, "Fear is excitement without the breath." *Is it possible that the fear of losing my freedom is pointing me toward the liberating realization that I do not have to sacrifice my freedom at all, only my definition of it?*

Something clicks. I've found a tiny crack of light in a maze of internal confusion, and I am going to follow it with everything I've got.

SHADOW WORK

We: Most human beings have no concept of shadow work, and even those that do may not have the courage or tools to voluntarily look into the dark crevices of their own psyche. Repressed traumas, inherited fear programs, unprocessed pain, and all sorts of other disturbing and uncomfortable revelations lie buried there, represented by the metaphorical "boogie man" of our collective human unconscious.

And yet—no matter how much we ignore, reject, and deny the shadow—it never disappears. In fact, quite the opposite is true. *The very fear that keeps us from looking at it is the same fear that feeds it.*

The greatest challenge we face when we embark into these realms of shadow work is that we are poorly prepared to navigate the emotions on the fear spectrum. Because we live in a culture that has no safe outlets for these parts of ourselves to express themselves, all the material we suppressed over the course of our lifetime has gotten stuck in us, as part of our shadow, and governs us unconsciously.

These suppression moments often happen from the best of intentions. A toddler falls, scrapes his knee, and bursts into tears. His mother instantly assures him, "It's okay, don't cry." This innocent desire from the mother to console her child is actually sending a very confusing message. The child doesn't feel okay at all, yet is being told that he should feel okay and that the emotional response he is having is invalid.

You can see why this terrain is so tricky. We each have countless examples of moments like this, moments that added up over time and created a deep rift in our ability to trust anything that hurts. We must learn how to genuinely not be okay, and let that be perfectly okay.

Looking at the shadow is no simple task. Once you open Pandora's box, you can't go back. There have been fleeting moments when we joke around that we wish we had stayed in blissful ignorance. But of course that is delusion, and the gifts we've received from facing the shadow far surpass the agony of it.

No one is exempt from the shadow. The question is, are you consciously engaging with its curriculum or trying to pretend it away?

If you've made it this far, you are likely feeling the call to dig into the rich soil of your own shadow. But how?

There are many modalities that we can use to become adept at collapsing the veil between our conscious mind and our subconscious mind.

What is this veil? It is a barrier that prevents us from being flooded with unconscious information that might impede our ability to survive or simply isn't necessary to be aware of. Our breath and our organs, for example, operate at a subconscious level. They do their job without us having to pay any attention to them, which is great. But our repressed traumas also hide out there, and if we wish to B Ξ Ϙ O M Ξ, we must begin to look at them.

When we shine the light of our awareness into the shadow of our unconscious, things that were shrouded in darkness become illuminated. This process usually requires us to alter our consciousness in some way in order to transcend the incessant chatter of the analytical mind and outsmart the overzealous bodyguard that is our ego, who is fervently guarding the threshold and keeping the veil intact in a valiant attempt to protect us from our shadow. This protection isn't a mistake. It's a survival mechanism to keep us from feeling things we haven't been equipped to feel. As children, these built-in defense mechanisms can be helpful and even lifesaving. But as adults, they become outdated and must be dismantled if we wish to evolve. In other words, it's time for the ego to retire. Some egos are willing to give up their posts fairly smoothly. Others put up a hell of a fight.

You may associate altered states with ingesting a substance, but that doesn't always have to be the case. Meditation, breathwork, orgasm, fasting, cold water, or death portal experiences (which can come through many avenues, including extreme sports or the passing of a loved one) are just a few examples of other "pattern interruptions" that will temporarily suspend our default state, override our defense mechanisms, and give us access to an altered perspective or sensation—even if just for a brief moment.

Because our personal, preferred modality to navigate the terrain of the shadow is the shamanic path of plant medicine, we—Azrya and Benjamin—will focus on this avenue. Not because it is the *only* way, but because it is the way we have personally explored to the deepest degree, and therefore, the path we can most authentically speak to.

WHEN DRUGS BECOME MEDICINE

The Brian C. Muraresku quote, "Die before you die," sums up the shamanic experience well, for it allows us to let our egos die, over and over again.

There's nothing more liberating than facing off with your worst fears and realizing they can't control you unless you resist them. This is the gift the medicines, altered states, and particularly Ayahuasca, give us: the gift of forcing us to surrender control.

Psychedelics and plant medicine predictably dissolve our concepts of reality and act as incredibly useful tools to access the energetic, psychospiritual and subconscious realms from which most human beings are astonishingly disconnected. Unlike drugs like cocaine, methamphetamines, opiates, and alcohol, which numb and suppress pain, thus keeping users in a state of escapism and avoidance, psychedelics and plant medicines—when administered in the right set and setting—do the opposite. They can take us right into the root of our pain, most of which boils down to the deeply engrained wound of separation.

In a Johns Hopkins study conducted in the 1970s, 67 percent of participants rated their guided, psychedelic experience among the top five most meaningful experiences of their lifetime. Now, for the first time since all clinical trials were shut down by Nixon during the War on Drugs era, new research is being funded and approved every day.

Because of their almost miraculous capacity to transform separation into connection, with psychedelics 10 years of psychotherapy can occur in a matter of hours. We firmly believe these medicines can provide accelerated solutions to some of the world's most urgent challenges.

So what do these mysterious substances do, exactly?

The answer to that is ever unfolding. From our personal experience, they do many extraordinary things, from facilitating neurogenesis to catalyzing full blown spiritual awakenings.

To boil it way down: When ingested in an intentional, responsible way (with professional facilitation), plant medicines help us identify where there's a lack or blockage of life-force energy, which we will go ahead and call love/light. If there's stagnancy, resistance, fear, trauma, or anything that's gotten stuck on the mental, emotional, physical, or spiritual planes, the medicine can start to loosen it and bring it to the surface. This creates space for more love/light to inhabit those pockets. That is when healing happens.

The medicine gives us the gift of temporarily collapsing our egoic defense mechanisms, actually facing the material of our subconscious that we have suppressed, and purging the fears associated with it. As we work with these ancient healing technologies, like building muscle over time, the nervous system learns to capacitate more and more love/light until, eventually, every moment—no matter how insignificant or mundane—is transformed into an expression of profound beauty, and our day-to-day life becomes the ultimate ceremony.

This "collapsing of the veil" between dimensions also collapses the veil between who we *think* we should be and what we *think* we should want, and reveals all we didn't know we wanted to be, do and have.

While we'd love to focus solely on the beauty of this work, we must also share that—like everything in our universe—the world of psychedelics and plant medicine also has its own shadow side. Peaking on LSD, a young man in our community thought he was invincible and fell off of a massive art installation at Burning Man, rendering him paralyzed from the neck down. There are horror stories of young women going to the jungle to work with shamans who end up sexually abusing them. As Ayahuasca becomes increasingly trendy, more and more people are serving the medicine who have no business facilitating it. Some have questionable motives, while others simply lack proper training and underestimate the seriousness of opening up someone's consciousness who might have a proclivity towards mental illness. With Ayahuasca in particular, there are contraindicated prescription medications such as antidepressants that make consuming the medicine life threatening, as well as a strict dietary protocol to follow before beginning the work in order to purify and prepare your system for the experience.

If you should ever feel the call to explore these realms, use discernment, consult your doctor, find direct referrals, and make sure your facilitator is properly vetted before you hand your life over to them.

Azrya: To me, working with Ayahuasca feels like picking up the phone and making a direct call to the consciousness of the Earth. She connects me back into the ancient intelligence of our original mother like an umbilical cord, and gives me direct access to the archives of infinite, sometimes highly visual information, stored in the cellular memory of my own DNA.

Bee: To me, Ayahuasca feels like a distinctly benevolent force of nature powerful enough to make me face off with the deepest parts of my ego and release the many fear-based attachments that have governed me consciously and unconsciously and relentlessly driven me toward seeking more and more control. She brings the warrior out in me, and I have deep respect for her tough-love teachings.

We: As our friend and medicine man Bear Heart taught us, our relationship to these "sacred teachers" begins with how we speak

about them. Instead of using the language of "taking" the medicine, which has the energy of extraction embedded in it, we say
"sit" with the medicine. Because that's what we're doing. Sitting
with the full spectrum of our human experience, in the classroom
of the plants, who have been around a lot longer than us and know
a thing or two about thriving on this planet.

Of course, there are many ways to heal and many ways to communicate with the divine. Plant medicine is a powerful avenue,
but again, it is not for everyone. When and if it's time to sit, the
medicine will call you. It often attracts people who have exhausted
every other resource, and while it is not addictive, it can become
a crutch if the work is not integrated properly after the ceremony.

Building a bridge from a peak, out-of-body, reality-dissolving,
metaphysical experience into our day-to-day lives is no easy task.
We require guidance, structure, and tools to really make the effects
last long after the ceremony has ended.

Many spiritual purists and hardcore meditation enthusiasts argue
that using an external substance on the path of enlightenment
is a shortcut. We have deeply reflected on this, truly examining
whether this sacred work could be an invalid method, attempting
to bypass decades of "real" work in order to take the fast track to
states of consciousness one can attain through meditation alone.
We've arrived at the following conclusion.

Imagine you are in a burning forest, and you have the option to
take the long way or the shortcut—which one would you take?

Probably the shortcut. If you look at the diseased state of our planet, our bodies, our minds, and our spirits, it's not hard to see that we are all living in a burning forest. We believe that burning forest is the result of generational trauma, manifesting itself today as environmental collapse, a health crisis with shocking statistics, and an obsession with *more-bigger-better-faster* that is driving our consumerist society toward extinction. The root of all of these issues? Fear.

So if fear is the root—what causes fear? Separation. From ourselves, each other, the planet, and most importantly, the benevolent intelligence of life itself.

The medicine can plug us back into the force field of love that sustains us at a soul level, without which we are nothing more than terrified little egos, trying to navigate a chaotic planet.

Think of psychedelics and plant medicines as biochemical, ancient technologies that activate dormant wisdom from within the molecules of your being and unlock the kind of information that can change the trajectory of your life forever.

Are you ready to die before you die?

HOW TO TRANSLATE TRANSCENDENCE

It's easy to focus on and sensationalize the actual psychedelic/plant medicine journey because of its metaphysical and extreme nature, but there can be no successful activation without proper integration.

Integration is what happens on the other side of a transcendental experience. Whether you're coming home from an incredible yoga retreat, breathwork workshop, MDMA assisted therapy session, or Ayahuasca ceremony, in each instance you've "transcended" your normal, day-to-day waking consciousness in a significant way, and tapped into an aspect of your spirit and your unconscious mind at a level previously inaccessible or unimaginable. In order for the benefits of that experience to last and become anchored into a new expression of your being in a permanent way, you will need to "integrate" the experience through cultivating practices that build a bridge between your expanded perspective and your waking reality.

The other component of integration that few people talk about is the strengthening of the actual nervous system to be able to capacitate the high vibrational information that is being translated into this third dimensional realm through the body as the vessel.

It is not at all uncommon for people who work with Ayahuasca and other psychedelics regularly to fry their nervous systems and exhaust their adrenals, like putting too much voltage through an electrical wire and blowing a fuse.

We—Az and Bee—have integrated a variety of integration tools, habits, and modalities into our daily lives that have become a default setting and will vary only slightly while traveling or for extra special occasions.

These include:

- mostly plant-based organic or non-GMO food
- no caffeine
- no alcohol
- no processed, fried, or fast food
- no refined sugar or wheat
- no soybean/canola oil
- no exposure to negative media of any kind
- movement such as hiking, stretching, strength training almost every day
- meditating
- journaling
- reading transformational books
- listening to uplifting and soothing music
- cold plunges
- sun exposure
- time outdoors
- quality time with family and friends
- solid sleep and permission to nap
- limiting screen time
- wearing blue blocker glasses and running the Flux app on our devices to reduce the strain on our eyes
- natural fabrics
- non-toxic soaps, cleaners, and beauty products
- less complaining
- lots and lots of gratitude

These are all essential ingredients for us to remain both tapped-in, grounded, and sane on the path of B Ξ Q O M I N G connected in a world that is mostly designed to keep us perpetually disconnected.

Awakening can happen in an instant, but embodiment happens in all the in-between moments of day-to-day life, and it requires the one ingredient that is non-negotiable when solidifying any lasting change: *consistency.*

That is also why Ayahuasca, or any psychedelic experience, is not a magic pill that will miraculously fix you. It's a tool. And only you can decide how you make use of that tool.

Because the Indigenous shamans who have worked with the plant teachers in a ceremonial context for generations have no real reference point for what a fast-paced, modern lifestyle with 24/7 internet access, artificially flavored "food," and incessant overstimulation feels like, integrating the medicine work is a massive gray area in which few people are well versed. It requires a unique person to have one foot in the shamanic realms and the other foot in the "matrix" of modern culture. Those who do learn, through trial and error, how to translate transcendence become bridge builders between the infinite and the finite. You could also say they become embodied.

Embodiment is really the alignment of your physical, mental, spiritual, and emotional signatures, to the point where they are all resonating at the same frequency. When no part of you is in conflict or contradiction within yourself, that is when you become fully integrated and embodied.

There are a lot of "spiritual" people who can spout esoteric concepts all day, but their lives, bodies, and bank accounts don't resemble much of what they preach. This is common, especially within the psychedelic and plant medicine community. Because these altered states blast us so swiftly out of the realm of the five senses and into the infinite, it's very easy to come back with the belief that you have it all figured out. We have certainly gone through this cycle many times in our study with mind altering substances, and it's taken much humility to learn that the real work only ever happens in the unglamorous moments of daily life, especially when no one is watching.

It's a delicate balance between KNOWING—with every fiber of your being—that you are a fractal of the universe with the ability to shape and mold reality through the power of your free will and, at the same time, remembering that you are a tiny speck of stardust floating through a 13.8-billion-year-old universe that is infinitely larger and more intelligent than you.

In the shamanic realms, time dissolves, truth has a million different faces, humans are gods and gods are humans, and nature is spirit and spirit is nature. The dance between fate and free will is never ending and always intersecting, and the paradox of a chosen destiny becomes increasingly hard to ignore.

Osho describes full embodiment (or integration) as that moment when the student is ready to throw the meditation practice away, for it is a tool that is no longer needed. Every moment becomes a living, breathing meditation. It's no longer a ceremony you attend once a year or even a daily practice you commit to for a lifetime.

To stabilize in a state of true KNOWING is to transcend all discipline and simply BE the living embodiment of the ever infinite, unknowable magic that is life itself, moving through you, unobstructed.

INVITATION #9:

- What parts of you are ready to die in order for you to step into the highest expression of yourself?

- What fears or resistance (shadow material) does that bring up?

- What is the opportunity on the other side of that fear/resistance?

- You don't have to attend a plant medicine ceremony to receive the benefits from altered states. We have provided a guided audio visualization exercise at **www.BEQOMING.me** for you to create your own ceremony called "The 5 Steps to Integrating Your Shadow and BEQOMING Fully Alive." You can also find the written instructions for this practice in the appendix. After you are done, give yourself some space and time to reflect & answer the following question:

What came up?

E.g. Resistance, pleasure, awareness, sensation, insight...write it down.

10

THE CHOICELESS CHOICE

"You can't buy devotion. Devotion can
only be gathered by showing up over and
over and over again with intention."

—Rebecca Campbell

180 DAYS

Bee: I've sat in more than 30 Ayahuasca ceremonies since meeting Azrya and have steadily made progress toward embodying my Truest Truth. On the other side of the Tulum death portal where I was able to liberate myself from deep fear-based attachments, the day-to-day joy and ease I am experiencing is at an all-time high, and I find myself hit with sudden bouts of heart-warming gratitude toward how beautiful my life is—a feeling that is very new to me.

But despite the intense shedding of so many outdated ways of being and the consistent purging of a lifetime of heaviness, a certain fog and chronic fatigue still remains that I can't seem to shake. In addition to that, my relationship with my son Steel still requires deep healing and I have no idea where to begin. This is why, when I am presented with the opportunity to work one-on-one with a very special medicine man who wishes to remain anonymous, and whom we will call Tao, I get on a plane with a list of intentions, ready to uplevel on the shamanic path once more.

One of the first things I observe about Tao is that he is incredibly meticulous with everything he does, and he sure takes his time. The impatient "let's hurry the fuck up and get to the point" part of me wants to judge him for his ways, but judgment isn't getting me anywhere. I have no choice but to surrender to his pace, watch, and learn.

Tao is a Brazilian son of Japanese parents. He began his spiritual journey at the age of six under a Japanese Shugendo master and has since developed a highly unique approach to the conscious work he calls The Bridge of Medicines, which honors and weaves ancient Eastern tantric traditions with shamanic teachings from the Andes to the Himalayas. On my path, I've met a whole laundry list of so-called spiritual guides, coaches, healers, shamans, and teachers, and right away I can tell that this guy is the real deal. I have hope that he might be the teacher I have been seeking for deeper study with the medicine.

"So what are your intentions?" Tao asks me, for what feels like the tenth time. I sometimes have the impression that he's sizing me up, but his facial expressions are impossible to read.

"I want to understand why I am—despite diligently doing so much inner work and taking such good care of myself—still feeling an underlying thread of constant depletion," I reply. "And I want to learn how to be a better father to my 14-year-old son Steel." Tao nods, remaining silent.

After lengthy preparations and a fire ceremony, Tao hands me my first cup of Ayahuasca. The medicine is light and doesn't really take me anywhere. So I drink a second cup. I came here to go deep, but still—nothing. After a long while of practicing patience, I want to ask for a third serving, but instead, I suddenly get hit with a wave of emotion and hear myself asking "Tao, will you help me?" It's a genuine, desperate plea.

He performs a lengthy energetic cleansing process on me using tobacco smoke. Afterwards, I feel a little better. "I think I'm ready for another cup," I say.

The moment the words leave my mouth, it's like a light switch is flipped within Tao as something very ancient and powerful inhabits him.

He stops, his face inches from mine. It is dark, his features are shrouded in shadows, but the way he's looking at me now, I can tell he's seeing well beyond my physical body.

"No," he says, his tone deliberate. "You don't need more medicine."

The way he sounds, it's like something else is speaking through him. I am taken aback by the intensity of his eyes. In the reflection of his pupils, I see into the depths of my soul.

"Benjamin," Tao continues, his words slow, steady, and ominous. "You are in serious trouble."

I instantly know that whatever he's about to tell me is the reason I came here. Every cell in my body is on high alert as I hang onto his every word.

"I am being shown that the energy of lust is at the root of all of your problems," he continues. "It is creating a distortion in your sexual energy that compels you to seek power outside of yourself, which is cutting you off from your spiritual self and draining your vital life-force energy. You have done a lot of damage by seeking validation through the conquest of women. You do not have the luxury of taking this lightly. Your spirit is suffering, and you are on the cusp of no return."

He speaks slowly and deliberately for the next few hours as I sit in silence KNOWING his every word is coming from the Truest Truth. He goes on to tell me that as long as I am carrying this energetic distortion, I will be unable to be the man I am aspiring to be, to serve the people I wish to serve. In no uncertain terms, he tells me that this is my last opportunity to address the issue before it's too late, and that if I don't, my children will inherit it. When I ask him where this distortion originated, he says it isn't clear, but it is likely from a karmic imprint left behind from one or many sexual experiences I have unconsciously engaged in.

"So what can I do to fix this?" I ask him.

He closes his eyes and goes into a meditation for what feels like an eternity, but is probably closer to 10 minutes.

"You will have to be celibate for 180 days, no more, no less." He finally tells me.

That means, not engaging in the energy of lust through thinking of or participating in any sexual acts for six months.

"Your chronic fatigue, brain fog, and even your relationship with your son will improve if you follow through with this," he assures me. "If you don't, your children will continue to carry the burden of this unresolved karma."

With every cell in my body, I believe him.

"Take some time to think about it," he says. "Decide if you are really ready to make this commitment."

"I don't have to think about it," I respond, without hesitation. "I already know I'm all in."

It's true, I feel with every fiber of my being that this is the final puzzle piece I've been searching for. Right there and then, I make the vow to myself and Tao and solidify it by giving him my ring with the family crest on it that means the world to me. "If I don't make it through, I am not worthy of wearing this," I tell him. "Hold onto it for me until I complete my 180 days of abstinence."

He agrees.

Tao urges me to consistently ask myself, *Who am I?* The journey of answering this question will lead me to shedding all illusory identity constructs that are being fueled by the energy of lust that defines so much of the collective enslaved masculine energy. "You are being initiated into understanding the shadow side of lust because you are here to guide many others toward liberation from it," he tells me. "If you don't clear this within yourself, it will be passed onto future generations to deal with."

His words resonate deeply for me. Instead of feeling any semblance of resistance in my body, I feel relief. I know that this is the kind of choice that eliminates all others. Committing to the 180 days feels liberating, like I can suddenly let go of this constant need to prove that I am worthy through performance and conquest. I intuitively know that this commitment will be my road to remembering my own wisdom and truly heal from a lifetime of being run by the *more = better* program that has bled into every corner of my life, and which has certainly showed up strongly in my pursuit of women.

We end up talking all night. Tao explains that ejaculation drains life force energy from the body, and retaining that energy for 180 days will create an internal "spiritual fire" that will purify the many karmic imprints I have collected from all the various sexual partners I had so casually indulged in during my single days. I am to work with meditation and breath to circulate any feelings of arousal up from my genitals to the top of my head, to fortify and fuel my connection to the spiritual dimensions. He agrees to continue to work with me, and I share that I see myself doing a deep-dive immersion with him at his retreat center in Peru before the 180 days are up.

The flight home from the retreat is rough. I am exhausted and my logical mind is trying to convince me I'm crazy. I have no idea how Azrya will take the news.

Azrya: The moment Benjamin walks through the door, I can tell something is different. He shares about the vow he made to Tao, and even before he's finished telling me the whole story, I already know it's right. It's almost as if this timeline that he chose when he made that vow was the final digit in a combination code lock that unlocked the full potential of our shared future. His devotion to his B Ξ Q O M I N G is encapsulated in that one decision, and it has made something available in him that I had previously only caught glimpses of; the truest, purest expression of his soul.

This is the man I choose to marry.

Together, we grieve the temporary sacrifice of our sexual connection. Our chemistry has been like a magnet from the very start, and now, from one day to the next, it's been completely eliminated. *Will what's left be enough to sustain us?* Both of us are confronted with this question, and while it's disorienting at first, we soon realize that removing sex from our relationship creates space for entirely new forms of intimacy to be cultivated. Just as we radically explored and celebrated the intensity of our explosive, orgasmic union with each other and Mars, we now get to dive deep into the opposite end of the spectrum and discover the ancient wisdom that reveals itself when all sexual energy is retained inside the body for an extended period of time.

In the absence of physical intimacy, a deeper desire for a different kind of presence from Bee reveals itself within me, and while it's vulnerable to share my needs, each difficult conversation we have brings us closer. All of the little moments are amplified now: feeling the warmth in his fingertips when he's gently running his hands through my hair while we watch a movie. His arms wrapping around me from behind in an unexpected hug while I'm standing at the sink. Steady eye contact when we speak. The joy exuding from his eyes when he's tickled by something funny I said. The more his system is nourished by retaining his life force, the more present he becomes. The more present he is, the more nourished I feel, the more any lingering parts of me that are questioning whether I can feel free in the lifetime commitment that is marriage are ready to transmute.

I am now at a place where I know I need to dissolve any last remnants of hesitation and truly go all in. But little tendrils of fear around losing my freedom still lurk in the recesses of my consciousness. I've taken this process as far as I can on my own. It's time to hire a coach who specializes in intimate partnership to help me find clarity about WTF my truth really is.

Within one session, the coach facilitates a breakthrough for me in which I am able to track the fear backward through my entire life and recognize how every single time I've followed my Truest Truth and spread my wings, it felt like I betrayed the hearts of those I love most. Unconsciously, I am bracing myself for the same situation to happen again and again.

Terrified of destroying our relationship and hurting Benjamin, I have resisted marriage because I've never trusted love to truly last. Sobbing, I recognize that I have the opportunity to transcend this unconscious loop and finally pass my hardest soul curriculum exam yet.

"Karma isn't about punishment, as most people think. It's about unconscious patterns that repeat themselves until you become aware of them and choose to break the loop. What makes them tricky to spot is that they feel deeply familiar," my coach Justin explains, "so when you're in them, they can almost feel like home." He's speaking directly to my soul. I have been struggling so much to discern what is my intuition speaking and what is my fear speaking. Like a PTSD victim, I was projecting heartbreak into the future because it was hardwired into my nervous system. And no wonder.

Never before has there been so much at stake, so much to lose. Never before have I been forced to see myself so clearly, in the reflection of another. Benjamin and I cannot hide our scars in the face of this love; it burns too bright. Everything must be illuminated, so that we may choose to overcome these deeply ingrained patterns and finally receive the lessons the universe has so expertly designed for us to receive.

After the session, I write the following insight into my journal:

Karmic Contracts

When you consciously choose to commit to collapse timelines held in place through karmic contracts, you initiate/catalyze an alchemical process in which the unconscious forces that govern fate begin to shift direction. Because these forces have become deeply ingrained in a predictable cycle/pattern that has manifested itself as a karmic loop for lifetimes, they take time to redirect. Just like you can't get a fast-moving cruise ship to make a sudden U-turn without tremendous effort and energy expenditure—the same is true for these patterns. It's not as simple as just "deciding" to. Your conscious mind is only about 15 percent of the equation. You need your unconscious to come onboard too.

As Carl Jung said, "**Until you make the unconscious conscious, it will direct your life and you will call it fate.**"

So how does one make the unconscious conscious?

All of the undigested material of the subconscious that has collected over the course of that pattern's life-span and could have the momentum of many lifetimes behind it will need to surface and be integrated.

This cannot occur all at once, as it would overload the nervous system with too much information to process. As Tao said to Benjamin during one of their follow-up calls, "Think of it as terabytes of information." So it comes in digestible chunks. In waves.

With karmic connections and contracts, we attract the people and circumstances that catalyze and accelerate this process. They act as mirrors for us to begin to access more of this material through their reflection. This is why the things that trigger us the most in others are the key to unlocking our deepest karmic curriculum. And this is especially true in intimate partnerships.

There's nowhere to hide.

In committed partnership, you have two cruise ships coming together to travel side-by-side toward a shared destination. At first it may seem effortless to stay on course because the intensity of early romance and its accompanying biochemical explosion of love hormones temporarily collapses the power of these fear-based forces. This is how nature intended it. It allows humans to bond on a level deep enough so that by the time their karmic curriculum surfaces, they will be much more likely to be willing to invest the time and energy to move through it together and evolve the species. Psychedelics and plant medicine often facilitate this temporary state as well, which is why MDMA therapy for couples is so powerful. It gives them a reprieve from the intensity and weight of their karma, so they can see clearly again and reconnect to the source of the love that is the truest expression of themselves and exists beyond all the pain, resentment, and broken trust.

But this is a temporary state designed only to give a reference point of what's possible so you can program it into the GPS of your cruise ships and come back to it when those karmic forces will inevitably begin to kick in and try to pry you apart.

This is when the real work begins.

It's so much easier to just give up on the shared destination when the going gets tough and try and find someone new, hoping that maybe this time it will miraculously "work out."

Depending on how much karmic curriculum there is, the intensity of the opposing forces will increase. Two very powerful people with strong creative energy and the capacity to make impact will likely have accumulated more karmic curriculum over the course of their souls' incarnations. How many "power couples" make it? Both parties are bringing a ton to the table. All their gifts and all their burdens.

Once that material surfaces, there's the choice. Stay together and transform the energy in a way that brings you closer, or give up and start over with someone new. Staying is not necessarily always the right answer. Sometimes the exam requires you to walk away in order to pass. Either way, you cannot escape your karma. The characters in the storyline might change, but the curriculum stays the same.

You can project blame on the other person all you want, but they are just your mirror pointing you to the unresolved material within yourself. Instead of saying "fuck you," the more useful response is "Thank you."

Yes, it will hurt. That's the point.

The pain wakes you up, it brings you alert by stripping you awake.

Hollywood would like us to believe that true love means promising you will never hurt the other. But on the path of B Ξ Ϙ O M I N G, you realize that someone who truly loves you will be willing to hurt you in the ways most conducive to your soul's highest evolution.

This willingness is part of the dojo of devotion that two people enter into on the path of awakened love and intimate partnership. No one else can hurt you in just the right way. No one else can get quite that close.

Will you turn and run, or will you stand and breathe?

That is **the relentless choice**. And making it, over and over again, is what will allow you to collapse the timelines generated by the karmic patterns of your subconscious. This is how you take the steering wheel of your destiny.

This is where fate and free will intersect.

As I begin to see the karmic contract more and more clearly, I am able to identify that Benjamin's fear-based ego, which, when threatened, had a reactive habit of resorting to over-seriousness and control mechanisms to protect itself, was perfectly designed to trigger my own fear-based ego and bring up doubt in my ability to feel truly free in the container of marriage. As a result, I had created a story that if he didn't evolve past those tendencies and learn to open his heart and trust, I might have my wings clipped and be forced to play out the same pattern of betrayal by eventually leaving in pursuit of "freedom." But true devotion isn't conditional. It doesn't say, "I will only love you if you are evolved." True devotion encompasses the full spectrum of another—from soul to ego, from balls to bones, from strengths to insecurities. It includes all of the beauty and all of the painful, messy bits. It doesn't shy away. It leans further in.

The epiphany comes when I finally realize that freedom is—at its core—always an inside job, and that **the ultimate freedom comes not from having all the options but rather choosing one option with every ounce of your being and pouring yourself entirely into making it the most profound thing it can be.**

Bee: While I wanted to turn and run away from the intensity of the death portal Azrya's uncertainty activated in both of us, ultimately, I found the courage to stand and breathe.

I can't say it was a choice. It was the Choiceless Choice. Like something much greater than me was choosing through me. As a result of surrendering to that force, my trust in the intelligence of life has deepened, and paradoxically, my trust in Azrya has too. Her willingness to stand in her doubt and be transparent about her process was agonizing, yet it forged in me a deep peace of mind, KNOWING that she will never withhold anything from me. She will never lie. She will never pretend. She is honest, to the core, no matter the cost. I can trust that beyond a shred of doubt, and it makes her word that much more meaningful when she does give it.

Our respect for each other deepened when we saw that in order to have a relationship that's true, we both needed to be willing to risk the relationship itself.

In a way, Azrya's fear of destroying me came true. She did destroy me. She destroyed the part of my ego that was still clinging to the fear-based control mechanism I've been enslaved to my whole life, the part of me that *needed* her lifelong commitment in order to feel safe and worthy. When I finally let that part of me begin to die, that's when I discovered that surrendering into something much greater than myself is where the real power lies. **Every surrender is a death, and over time, you just get good at it.** When people ask me about my journey into trust, I describe it like watching the process of boiling water. For a long time, it looks like nothing is happening. Then the bubbles suddenly erupt and the water is boiling. The same has been true for my process of B Ξ Ϙ O M I N G. It happened very slowly, and then all at once.

The paradox is that while I've come so far on the journey from my head to my heart, I also know I am only just beginning. Every death is a layer of the onion coming off.

In the same way Azrya was an integral part of my spiritual evolution in the sense that she forced me to surrender in ways I didn't know were possible, my unwavering commitment to loving Azrya *no matter what* also destroyed something in her. It forced the part of her that was looping in an old wound of betrayal and an outdated definition of freedom to relinquish its own fear-based defense mechanisms and let them die into a depth of devotion previously unimaginable.

That same unimaginable devotion catalyzes in me a deep desire to have a child with Azrya. Even without the promise of forever that I had previously been so attached to, the Choiceless Choice compels me to get my vasectomy reversed and open the channel for a child to come through. Not because "I" want to. But because "I" have simply gotten out of the way of love's intelligent plan. And it feels so fucking good.

Of course, the moment I truly let go of needing any guarantees, on a quiet, chilly morning in a hotel room in Austin, Azrya shares with me under the covers that she wants nothing more than to get legally married. "I realize now: all it takes is everything," she whispers, snuggling up against my chest, her breath warm on my skin. "And I am finally ready to give you my everything."

Her voice is quiet, but rich with a KNOWING I've never felt in her before.

When you genuinely surrender what you think it should be, you get *everything you didn't know you wanted*.

Something that is Truly True, not forced.

FINDING EACH OTHER IN A NEW TRUTH

We: We can't argue with the KNOWING. Like trying to keep a beach ball underwater, suppressing it requires a huge amount of energy, for it is always trying to break through the surface and reveal itself. Most of our lives are spent wrestling with the beach ball, trying to keep it submerged and under control at all costs. The act of surrendering, of letting go and allowing the KNOWING of our Truest Truth up and out, may seem terrifying. It may threaten to annihilate us. Rest assured, it will. But only the parts of us that need to die will die.

Like the caterpillar relinquishing its form in the cocoon in order to emerge on the other side as a butterfly, the Truest Truth will lead us through an intense transmutation toward our highest evolutionary potential. This shedding, stripping, awakening might not always be pretty, but it will certainly be beautiful.

Sometimes the Truest Truth will give us *everything we knew we wanted*. More often, it will reveal everything we didn't know we wanted. When we are in alignment with it, "There is no inner contradiction, no war between what you are doing and what you think you should do"—to use Krishanmurti's words.

Bee: When I reflect on the subject of having a child, I can see how it gifted me with the powerful distinction between what my ego was convinced my truth was (not wanting to have another child under any circumstances) and the Truest Truth. The distinction lies in the "I" versus the "WE."

The truth of my "NO" came from a selfish place, an "I" place, in that it was an expression of what I believed served the best interest of my personal preferences. **But the Truest Truth is not about what I do or do not think I want; it's not about defending what I thought my truth was supposed to be; it's about what Love wants, beyond preference.** Surrendering myself to an intelligence far greater than my own limited lens on reality is an act of devotion that unclogs my channel to source.

For me, learning the art of cord cutting and committing to six months of celibacy were powerful techniques to allow me to undo much of the damage I had unconsciously done to my life-force energy through several years of promiscuity. Leading up to Peru, Tao instructed me to review every single sexual encounter I've ever had where I was out of integrity and infused with the shadow of lust and "cut" the energetic cord that was created through the act, thus taking back what is mine and giving back what is not. I also cut cords with anyone I've ever had conflict with, including business relationships.

This practice untethers unhealthy attachments that may still be linking us to previous partners, whether sexual or not, and restores our body's capacity to retain its own life-force energy, versus it leaking into other people. While the logical mind operates within the construct of space and time, our energy bodies exist in the quantum field where all things are occurring simultaneously and where energetic cords may still be entangled with previous partners until intentionally severed. The process also forced me to dismantle my sexual identity and reevaluate what masculinity truly meant to me.

The purpose of the celibacy was similar to the cord cutting process, in that it severed the exchange of my life-force energy, even with Azrya, for the purpose of purification and regeneration. Combined with powerful breathing techniques, meditations, and over 20,000 mantras, the 180 days of abstinence allowed my energy body to repair itself by having the opportunity to recharge its depletions at a cellular level. The chronic fatigue, brain fog, and memory loss I had been battling began to reverse themselves over the course of the protocol, and my spiritual connection strengthened. It was incredibly empowering to watch my connection with Azrya deepen, despite not "providing" in the bedroom the way I've always believed a "real" man should.

Once the energy could flow freely through that channel, with it came a deep KNOWING that a child wants to come through whose name Azrya and I both instantly KNEW would be Choice Bequer. When I gave myself over to that KNOWING and allowed myself to make contact with his spirit, being fully available, without attachment, for that child to come into this world, it became *everything I didn't know I wanted*. Whether the energy of Choice wants to come through as a child in this life or the next, or as a project or mission that Azrya and I co-parent is not up to us to decide.

Regardless, we get to love it with everything we've got.

For instructional Cord Cutting *video, please see www.B Ξ Q O M I N G. me/tools.*

Azrya: I wasn't authentically able to stabilize in the KNOWING that I was ready to make a lifetime commitment to Bee because there was interference in our frequencies. Like a radio signal that is coming in and out, our unresolved karmic curriculum needed to be brought to the surface of our awareness and the gifts contained within it, integrated. Only then could I finally stabilize in the KNOWING.

The 180 days of celibacy was a crucial component for that to be possible because it gave us time to untangle our deeply intertwined energetic bodies and come back into sovereignty within ourselves. In the ensuing clarity, I was able to finally embody what my heart had been initiating me into accepting from the very beginning: that devoting myself to Benjamin for life was everything I didn't know I wanted.

And that, in fact, this act of devotion to one man was no different than being in devotion to the vast intelligence of life itself, for they are one and the same.

Sweet Surrender
by Azrya

I humbly bow
at the altar of this love
giving up all pretenses
and all defenses
against the immensity of its power.
Like an ant peering at the sun
and trying to comprehend its magnitude
I kneel before this love

surrendering my bleeding heart to its divine will.
And finally choosing
to let it have its way with me.
To stop fighting
analyzing
questioning
and simply allow it to overtake me.
To annihilate me
splay me wide open
and scoff at my preferences
my demands
my misbelief that I have any control over the karmic immensity
of this relentless love.
Beaten to the ground by my own fear
of betraying this love
I realize now
you can never lose something you don't actually own
and so I bow
gratitude dripping from my burning pores
stripped awake
wide awake
yet again
as I surrender the "I"
to B Ξ Q O M Ξ
the WE.

THE SACRED K(NO)W

We: One could argue that the entire BΞQOMING journey of personal transformation is to remember, trust, and then live according to our KNOWING. Of course, there are caverns of doubt that stand between us and the KNOWING, and it is important to realize that we can't will the doubt to disappear; it has to happen spontaneously, organically.

If we are feeling doubt, we must lean into it. **The doubt is there to teach us something.** It is there to illuminate the path to the KNOWING by showing us what's in the way of it. Commit to the doubt fully—don't resist it. **If you don't yet know, then don't yet know—but with 100 percent certainty.** The suffering happens when we think we should already KNOW and are making ourselves wrong for not being there yet.

You are always exactly where you are supposed to be. How do you KNOW?

Because that's where you are.

The KNOWING also manifests itself as The Sacred K(no)w, which creates the effortless "nos" to the things not in alignment with the KNOWING. This applies to all things and is very practical because, as Gary W. Keller and Jay Papasan say in *The One Thing,* "One yes must be defended by a thousand nos."

For example, you just quit your job to finally pursue your passion, and then your old boss offers you a promotion in hopes of getting you back. The Sacred K(no)w will help you pass on the seductive paycheck. Or you are finally ready to lose the extra 20 pounds of weight you've been carrying around for too many years. The Sacred K(no)w that you are worthy of feeling vibrant in your skin will allow you to say no to the Oreo crunch cheesecake someone left in the cafeteria. Perhaps you're in a great long-term relationship but you're moving through a rough patch. When a beautiful woman hits on you at the bar, The Sacred K(no)w that your partner's heart is the most precious thing you've been given the opportunity to cherish will help you politely decline her advances.

You may have heard the famous personal development quote: "How you do anything is how you do everything." Commitment is available in every action, whether it be brushing our teeth, taking the trash out, or building an empire. The more committed we are to the moment, the more present we are with it, the more time will seem to disappear and magic be revealed.

Being committed to the KNOWING of your Truest Truth and the many Sacred K(no)ws that come with it is a path of radical self-awareness and mastery, and it is liberating. Richard Rudd says in *The Gene Keys*: "As you allow the energy of commitment to act itself out in the world, you begin to realize that an energy separate from your body is moving through you." To fully commit is to abolish half-heartedness and go all in, whether it be to a relationship, a project, a mission, a philosophy, or a way of life. We are not talking about rigidity here. "Commitment is akin to trust, which can neither be forced nor willed," Richard Rudd explains. "To commit is also to surrender. Rather than expending a huge effort to maintain your commitment, you simply surrender to it. Sometimes if you feel a lack of commitment, it's because you need to surrender even more deeply into your process."

He continues to talk about the cycles of commitment and how they have their own intelligence. If we are truly committed, we will KNOW when the cycle is over and then be equally committed to letting go and committing to something new.

In our case, committing to a shared lifetime had to be anchored in a KNOWING that we were committed to seeing the cycle of our love through to the end and wholeheartedly believing that the end will be death itself, while also trusting that if the cycle should end before then, we'd both KNOW in our hearts why and honor that.

This is perhaps the ultimate paradox of commitment. To be so devoted to the commitment that you are willing to energetically "burn the ships at the shore" as Columbus allegedly did, while simultaneously being so surrendered to the intelligence of life itself that you do not cling to something long after the time has come to let it go.

INVITATION #10:

- Evaluate the most intimate relationships in your life. What might the karmic contracts be between you? What challenges are present?

- How connected do you feel to your Truest Truth and your KNOWING?

- Discerning intellectual knowing from KNOWING is a practice that requires the silencing of internal and external noise to fully come online. We have prepared a guided meditation called *Finding the KNOWING* for you to develop this ability to discern between the two, by listening deeply to your inner voice. Visit www.BEQOMING.me/tools to access the content. After you are done, free-flow in writing about your experience.

11

IN LOVE WE TRUST

"I don't know what Truth is.
But I know what Love feels like."

—Tao

Bee: Azrya and I decide to have our official wedding on the last day of my 180 days of celibacy. We put the date on the calendar, and next thing I know, I'm scheduling my vasectomy reversal procedure. Even as I'm pushed out of the surgery center in a wheelchair with stitches in my balls, hopped up on pain meds, I have a deep KNOWING that this entire process is divinely guided and my heart feels full. Everything is flowing beautifully between Azrya and I and we are closer than we've ever been, but my personal process with Ayahuasca is not yet complete. While my unhealthy attachments to my sexual identity have transmuted and left me feeling empowered as a man in an entirely new way, I am still mid-initiation, and it won't be over until I complete my three week "dieta" in the Peruvian jungle.

A dieta is a deep dive study with Ayahuasca during which you have no communication with the outside world. You spend most of your days in isolation and silence, remove all salt from a diet that consists entirely of rice, lentils, and boiled plantains, and are given just enough to keep going. For a minimum of 10 days, you sit in an Ayahuasca ceremony every second night. The rest of the time, you are alone. The idea is to remove all input so you have nowhere to hide from yourself. All of your physical and emotional toxins, attachments, traumas, and unresolved shadow material will begin to come up and out.

My three-week initiation in Peru is facilitated by Tao and designed to end five days before the 180th day of celibacy, the date of which will now forever be marked as the day Azrya and I got married. Tao instructs me not to use any soap or toothpaste for the duration of the experience. I am only allowed to bathe in a river and wash myself with leaves. By day eight, I stop eating entirely; the lack of salt has killed my appetite.

Dietas are designed to break down your ego, and mine certainly puts up a good fight. Confronted with the deepest, darkest aspects of my fear-based attachments and insecurities, I feel naked and alone for the vast majority of the experience. Having two camera men with me to capture the experience on film only amplifies the intensity.[4] Profound grief pours through me as my heartbroken inner child finally has the opportunity to feel all the things it never had the courage to feel. Clinging to my purge bucket for dear life,

---

4   Visit *www.B≡QOMING.me/film* to watch Benjamin's shamanic initiation in Peru.

I question all of it: the medicine, my purpose, and everything I thought I knew about reality.

After the jungle, my initiation continues in the Andes at an elevation of 14,000 feet (4,500 meters), where we stay in small dirt huts with no electricity or heat for five days. The dizzying altitude and bitter cold breaks what is left of my physical resilience down until I am so exhausted, I can barely see straight.

On the other side of the breakdown, a new version of me begins to—very timidly—emerge in the form of spontaneous creative expression and an expanded state of awareness. Spoken word poetry starts flowing through me in response to the question Tao had instructed me to contemplate six months prior: *Who are you?*

Here are a few lines I scribbled in my journal while in Peru.

> Through the reflection of others
> Especially those closest to me
> Especially my Queen Bee
> I see "the man that God meant, when God meant me"[5]
> I faintly see the King I never dreamt I could be
> I'm B Ξ Q O M I N G the man I was designed to be
> A man on a journey of B Ξ Q O M I N G Love
> Of remembering who I already Bee
> Of remembering there is only ever
> WE

---

5   Inspired by Morgan Snyder.

This is a lifelong journey. Sometimes it feels like I have been on it for eons; other times it feels like I am only just scratching the surface. Perhaps both are true. What matters is that the path is clear, and as I learn from Tao, humility is the first door.

"In ways you will never understand, I got through this dieta because of you," I tell Azrya after we finally speak again.

It's true. My love for Azrya acted like a magnet, pulling me through the most grueling of times. Visions of us standing at the altar kept me going even when everything inside of me wanted to give up. All of the accumulated heartbreak caused by the rift between me and some of my oldest friends rose to the surface during my time in Peru, and I decided to open my heart to all of them again by inviting them to the wedding even though I had firmly decided against it. Having been so deeply judged by some of them in the past, it feels like a risk, but my Truest Truth urges me to let go, forgive, and trust love.

As I deepen my commitment to the spiritual path, I learn that shifting our operating system from fear to love is not just a conceptual idea. There's a cellular transformation that must take place for it to come into full embodiment. It's a "stripping down to rebuild" process, in which—over time—every building block of our mental, emotional, and physical self must be filtered through the light of awareness and then integrated through the tangible micro-decisions we make every single day.

I'll be the first to admit that I've been one to get enamored with the idea of the "quick fix" solution. When I first heard of Ayahuasca, it sounded like a magic pill I could take that would just deliver me all the answers. The illusion that we can find answers outside of ourselves is a hard one to transcend, and my dieta forced me to face off with the deepest part of my psyche that deeply yearned to be "fixed" through some external source—whether it be the medicine or a healer—rather than trusting in my own internal wisdom and innate wholeness. The truth is that the path to radiant health and vitality on all levels is much more humbling, in that it takes time, consistency, and relentless commitment. It's taken me years to clear the brain fog and open up my channel to Source, and I am just now tasting the real rewards that come from this level of consciousness while also realizing how much further I still have to go.

The ultimate paradox of this path is that "**there's further to go and nowhere to get**," as Azrya always says. We must seek to B Ξ Ǫ O M Ξ, only to realize that our very seeking is what prevents us from arriving in the perfection of every single moment anew.

MARRIED AGAIN, FOR THE FIRST TIME

Azrya: I have no intentions to get an official white wedding dress. I'm not traditional, remember? Bee and I decided to keep this casual and wear something comfortable. My beach dress will do just fine.

Next thing I know, my shamanic maid-of-honor Blu and I are pulling up outside of a bridal shop I randomly found on Yelp. We're just here for fun, to have the experience of trying on some ridiculous dresses, not to buy anything. After all, one of our favorite scenes of all time is from the movie *Bridesmaids*, which involves very fancy dresses and projectile diarrhea caused by an unfortunate food poisoning incident. For us, that scene is a true classic, and we can't pass up on the opportunity to play a little and see if my tattoos make good accessories for lace and tulle.

Five minutes after we step foot in the bridal shop, I fall head over heels in love with the first dress I try on. Blu is in tears at how perfect it is. Everything about it just clicks.

Shit. This just turned into a proper wedding.

With Bee off the grid in Peru, I am pretty much in charge of pulling together the logistics for the big day, and as the guest list steadily expands, so does my overwhelm. Before I know it, I am drowning in details. Bee is traversing the shamanic realms while I'm on the phone with customer service, trying to make sure our rose gold utensils will ship in time. We've officially traded places.

During this time, I feel the strong urge to reconnect with Benjamin's mom after a long period of separation. I know I'm not her favorite person, but we are about to officially carry the same last name and I want things to feel good between us. When I visit her for lunch, I show her a picture of the wedding dress, and just like that, everything changes.

I'm so used to Ayahuasca being the medicine that heals all I would have never thought this time, the medicine would come in the form of my wedding dress. But like magic, the moment Bee's mom lays eyes on the white lace, her heart opens to me. Perhaps it's because of her love for tradition. Perhaps it's because suddenly my union with her first-born son feels real in a way she could never receive before. Whatever it is, her eyes light up, and before I know it, she's generously pouring her energy into helping me turn this casual "backyard gathering" into a proper production. As we spend quality time picking out flowers and deciding what size dance floor to order, we deepen our trust and put the past behind us. I enjoy needing her help, and she enjoys being needed. All of the tension between us dissolves, and I am so grateful to receive her nurturing, motherly love from this truly authentic place. It finally feels safe to lean into this woman who gave birth to the man I love most.

Relieved and excited, my overwhelm quickly turns to ease. Everything continues to click into place, and before I know it, the big day has arrived and I am standing in front of a gorgeous arch covered in white roses, staring into the eyes of the man who is more than everything I didn't know I wanted. He is the dream I didn't have the imagination to dream.

True to form, our ceremony is packed with twists and turns. Benjamin's daughter Gysel is the surprise officiant, and Benjamin's ex-wife Grisel is his "best man." But the real surprise comes when we exchange our vows and Bee blows me away with a fully memorized eight-minute-long spoken word poem that sounds like it was written by an expert poet.[6]

---

6   Watch our wedding vows at *www.BΞϘOMING.me/we*.

I then surprise him by performing the very first song I wrote him, aptly named *Honey Bee*. With the audience laughing and crying every step along the way, Gysel closes the ceremony by asking each of us whether we declare ourselves ready and willing to protect, nourish, and celebrate the beauty and wholeness of each other's hearts.

We do.

Finally, Benjamin places his thick, warm hand on my delicate neck and gently yet firmly pulls me close for a mind-melting kiss that makes everything else fade into the background, leaving only him and I, wrapped in the embrace of a small eternity, completely enveloped in the force field of our timeless love.

We dance and celebrate for hours, surrounded by the purest of intentions and well wishes, then end the night by burning the bracelet Tao gave Bee—thus closing the six-month container of celibacy.

After six months of barely touching, the time finally comes for us to reunite intimately. Although we have both deeply trusted this entire process, small, human fears have crept in this past six months. *What if it's different now? What if the sexual chemistry is offline for good? What if the machinery doesn't work anymore?*

Any fears about our chemistry fading are completely obliterated the moment we crawl under the sheets and allow the energy to flow. The anticipation and build-up heightens the sensation of lips brushing skin, mouths tasting tongues, and bodies finding their way home to each other in pure devotion for what almost feels like the first time while still being deeply familiar. We are perfectly in-sync as we re-discover and devour every inch of each other, completely present with every drop of passion, milking the moments of push and pull, of tension and release, of domination and surrender. Our sexual connection is like a rocketship, unflinching in its KNOWING that these bodies were perfectly designed to catapult each other into the most sublime sensations of ecstatic bliss.

As one of the lines in my song goes, "I am the lock and you are the key." That line is quite literal.

SPREADING THE LOVE

The following morning, Grisel excitedly greets Bee and I in the kitchen.

"Something really incredible happened with Steel last night," she says. "As he was getting ready for bed he suddenly stopped and told me, 'Mom. I'm in a meditative state. I don't know why, but I feel... reborn.'"

Our eyes widen. That language is very out of left field for Steel, who rarely communicates about his feelings.

We ask Grisel what time he shared this, and she tells us it was around 10 p.m.; *just after we burned the celibacy bracelet*. Steel has also been going through a profound transformation over the 180-day period, just as Tao had boldly predicted, but this was a powerful confirmation.

It might be hard to see the connection between a father's abstinence and his children's well-being if you're seeing them as separate entities. If you can transcend the lens of separation and acknowledge the energetic and karmic interconnectedness we share with our fellow humans, especially our blood family, then it makes sense that the powerful intention infused into Bee's commitment of devotion would have a tangible, spiritual impact on his own children. We are all wowed and grateful.

Two days after the wedding, I put my wedding dress on again, except this time I combine it with a pair of black leather combat boots. We pile the remaining flowers into the trunk of our blood red '53 Buick Roadmaster, stop by the post office to drop off our marriage license, and then drive to Venice, California, with the top down, where we proceed to hand out all the flowers to dozens of people passing by.

Blessings ooze from my every pore. After two years of intense shedding, stripping, breaking, and transforming, I've landed in a place of pure joy. A chapter has ended, and a new one is beginning. I know that all will work out as long as we remember to always and forever...

Trust love.

THE PRACTICE OF B Ξ Q O M I N G

"If not us, who? If not now, when?"

—John F. Kennedy

We: At the very beginning of this book we spoke about **Kintsugi,** the Japanese art of putting broken pottery pieces back together with gold—built on the idea that by embracing flaws and imperfections, you can create an even stronger, more beautiful piece of art.

Perhaps now you are beginning to feel the visceral breaking open that the path of B Ξ Q O M I N G requires. Even if it's still intellectual at this point and hasn't penetrated into your emotional body yet, just the act of sincerely contemplating the answers to the questions we've posed throughout this book will catalyze a powerful shift, from the inside out. For some of you, that shift will be sudden. For others, it will be gradual, gaining momentum over time.

B Ξ Q O M I N G is a state of being that is not fixed, but always fluid. The moment we think we've got it dialed, we inevitably get tested because life is designed that way. That's its gift to us. By poking and prodding relentlessly at our most tender wounds, life gives us moment after moment to choose a new experience for ourselves— from the inside out, not the outside in.

Choosing to step fully onto the path of B Ξ Q O M I N G does *not* mean we don't feel pain. In fact, the opposite is often true. It means we stop resisting the inevitable pain that is part of our natural human experience and embrace it fully and "die into it."

The path of B Ξ Q O M I N G is not for the faint of heart. Many will begin walking it, all bright eyed and bushy tailed—but most will fall off as soon as the curriculum steps it up and the emotional intensity of the death process skyrockets. For while B Ξ Q O M I N G is free, the cost is high. Too high for most.

B Ξ Q O M I N G requires giving no less than everything. But it also gives us *everything we didn't know we wanted.*

Remember, we're not talking about the shiny Ferrari or the perfect beach body here. We're talking about the real shit. **The deep satisfaction of radiating aliveness from every pore of our being, simply by sincerely savoring the present moment.** The kind of self-worth and internal security that nothing external can ever deliver or threaten. The capacity to keep our heart open *no matter what* and truly learn to become the embodiment of love in every moment. The willingness to remember just how whole and perfectly imperfect we already are, right now, without anything needing to change.

And finally—the unwavering trust in the benevolence of an intelligent universe that is conspiring to serve our greatest growth with every moment. How do we get there?

The journey of B Ξ Q O M I N G never really ends, it's more of a practice than a finish line. The process matures us to be less focused on goals, and more immersed in life. Like learning to drive a car, we begin to notice that it requires less focus and effort, and eventually it seems to be happening almost on its own. This is what we call "anchoring it in."

The path requires us to strip ourselves awake by looking within and systemically facing off with every last shred of fear-based attachment we carry inside of us. It demands complete and utter devotion to the present moment, no matter what that moment feels like; a challenge that our mind and our biology will relentlessly attempt to derail us from achieving over and over again in the name of self-preservation.

With practice and presence, we learn to anchor a vibrational set point into our being that begins to define us more than all the noise in our heads.

BƎQOMING UNFUCKWITHABLE

When doubt and fear no longer distort our KNOWING, we enter the realm of BƎQOMING Unfuckwithable. As we shared at the beginning of this book, this word and our use of it refers to a state, a frequency that we can learn to attune ourselves to. It's what we might mistake for "confidence"—but an evolved version that is based on deep internal wholeness and lightness of being. Confidence is so often attached to external things, such as status, appearance, influence, and competence, and often reveals itself to be a thin veneer, covering a medley of deep-rooted insecurities.

The Unfuckwithable state, on the other hand, comes from a deep inner centeredness. It doesn't necessarily always express itself as inner peace, although it often feels very much like that. But it also embraces the opposite of inner peace. It embraces chaos, devastation, and death with the same reverence as it embraces inner peace, for it knows "this too shall pass." So it devours all of it, the peace and the war, gratefully, humbly soaking in every last drop of sensation—beyond the paradigm of preference, beyond the paradigm of positive and negative, beyond any and all labels or stories of good and bad, beautiful and ugly, right and wrong. From that place, we become equipped to *respond* to injustice rather than *react*, and can then take appropriate action to evolve the situation. Not from a place of resisting, repressing, or denying What Is, but from a place of truly allowing What Is to penetrate us to the core.

Someone on the sincere path to B Ξ Q O M I N G Unfuckwithable doesn't need life to be easy. This path is about celebrating life for being anything *but* easy.

Those who embody even just a smidge of Unfuckwithability tend to B Ξ Q O M Ξ highly magnetic because it is a frequency that needs nothing external in order to be powerful. Such people radiate pure presence, which is the access point to infinite possibility. They exude what the Buddha meant when he said "be a light unto yourself." They are that light, and it spills from their every pore in unlimited supply.

B Ξ Q O M I N G is not just a hip way to "get woke" and stay up to date on the latest health and wellness trend. B Ξ Q O M I N G is a path to true sanity. And ironically, it requires us to lose our minds first. Or at least, to lose the identification with our mind that drives so much of the anguish we face in our modern culture today.

B Ξ Ọ O M I N G will always require us to confront death as a prerequisite for rebirth.

With escalating pandemics, Black Lives Matter, global warming, political disarray, and the various other disasters currently wreaking havoc on our planet, you could say our entire world is urgently being invited into a collective initiation of B Ξ Ọ O M I N G. And since the collective is nothing more than a collection of individuals, it makes sense that—once we embrace the reality of interconnectivity—this death/rebirth process is occurring in our personal lives as well. As on the macro, so on the micro. None of us are exempt.

Our entire consumerist society crumbles in the face of those dedicated to B Ξ Ọ O M I N G Unfuckwithable. An individual who is so utterly self-sustained becomes a radical rarity in a world designed to keep us trapped in the illusion of lack. Which is why nothing in our education systems prepares us for it. We are sold a frozen TV dinner version of one-dimensional "happiness" and spend our lives grasping for it like a very confused dog chasing its tail until it falls over from sheer exhaustion.

That exhaustion is a gift. A portal. An invitation to let go of the illusion of separation and awaken to something much more beautiful and true that only we can define, through the power of our own KNOWING.

THE JOURNEY OF BEQOMING

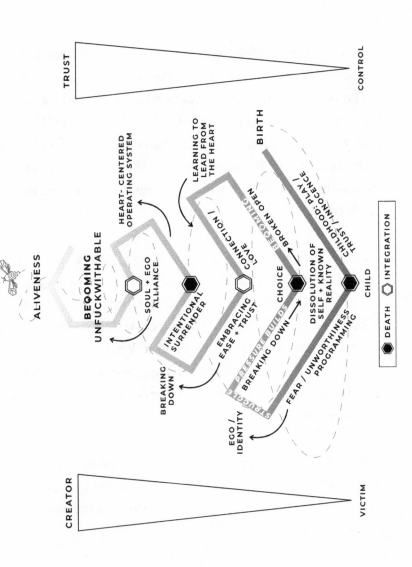

TRUST

CONTROL

CREATOR

VICTIM

DEATH INTEGRATION

ALIVENESS

BEQOMING UNFUCKWITHABLE

HEART-CENTERED OPERATING SYSTEM

LEARNING TO LEAD FROM THE HEART

SOUL + EGO ALLIANCE

INTENTIONAL SURRENDER

BREAKING DOWN

CONNECTION / LOVE

EMBRACING EASE + TRUST

BEQOMING

BROKEN OPEN

CHOICE

BIRTH

CHILDHOOD: PLAY / INNOCENCE / TRUST

DISSOLUTION OF SELF + KNOWN REALITY

CHILD

PRESSURE BUILDS

STRUGGLE

BREAKING DOWN

EGO / IDENTITY

FEAR / UNWORTHINESS PROGRAMMING

THE JOURNEY OF BEQOMING

This graphic shows the broad strokes of the archetypal BEQOMING journey. Each of the death portals signifies a pivotal moment where some aspect of the known self and identity must fall away to create space for the new version that is emerging. Each of these deaths is a choice point and must be grieved appropriately.

As we consciously shed the old, fear-based attachments; embrace our soul's curriculum; and embody a new, heart-centered O.S., the cycle repeats itself but with greater and greater ease. As we integrate our unconscious fears and our frequency harmonizes with life, the ego learns to loosen its grip on the known identity, and the death / rebirth moments are seen as gifts from the universe, offering us the opportunity to shape and mold who we choose to

BEQOME through the power of choice.

FIND THIS CHART + MORE RESOURCES AT BEQOMING.me/resources

CONCLUSION

YOUR INVITATION

"We need only look with different eyes
to realize we are already there."

—Charles Eisenstein

We: Don't think of this book as a collection of chapters that you just finished reading. Think of this book as a portal into a new version of yourself. Think of it as taking the red pill. You are now at a choice point moment, where you can wake up out of a dream and begin assimilating an entirely new version of reality.

Where to begin integrating all you have received in this book? No doubt, the 40-billion-dollar personal transformation industry is booming. Everywhere you turn, life coaching programs, yoga studios, and healthy eating trends are popping out at you. The wave of consciousness sweeping this planet is part of a beautiful blossoming, which has been prophesied by ancient cultures for thousands of years as being the time when humanity has the opportunity to awaken to the truth of interconnectivity and find its way back home after a long and painful excursion into the realms of separation.[7]

That said, whether you've been on a journey of B≡QOMING for a long time or you're just beginning, let's be real: it can be really fucking overwhelming to know which of the many possible paths to take.

There's the path of meditation, which in and of itself has a whole plethora of offshoots, that include everything from white-turbaned Kundalini chanting practices to OneTaste, whose central focus is female orgasm and sexuality.

There's the plant medicine and psychedelic assisted therapy path, which exists in a constantly shape-shifting gray area and comes with a whole slew of unanswerable questions, risks, and charlatan shamans.

There's the unregulated coaching and retreat path, where choosing between Landmark Forum, Mastery in Transformational Training, or good old Tony Robbins, not to mention the thousands of other options, can make your head spin. And then, of course, there's the

---

7   Inspired by: https://charleseisenstein.org/essays/the-three-seeds.

endless contradictions between all of these different avenues. The vegans are certain their way of being is the most compassionate and sustainable. The Keto enthusiasts are convinced that animal products will revolutionize health. Everywhere you turn in the wellness and spirituality departments, there's arguments for every side that sound totally convincing.

Truth is: We don't have *the answer*. All we know is what works for us, and even that is continually evolving. In the Appendix, you'll find a simplified version of a powerful practice that you can apply directly to your own experience called, "The 5 Steps to Integrating Your Shadow and B Ξ Q O M I N G Fully Alive."

For a comprehensive list of authors and books, podcasts, and articles that had a profound impact on us, visit *www.B Ξ Q O M I N G. me/resources.*

Yoga, exercise, meditation, choosing love over fear, opening over closing, healthy eating, nourishing sex, devoted daily practices, plant medicine, personal development, or any of the other modalities we talk about in this book are all practices and tools, not some distant destination you arrive at. Similarly, B Ξ Q O M I N G Unfuckwithable is a practice. Everyday life is generous enough to provide you with the curriculum and offers infinite invitations to practice being in that state. Just like any other practice, the more you consciously engage in flexing that muscle, the easier and easier it gets to stabilize there.

We believe there are no accidents in this world, and it is not an accident you found this book. Our invitation to you, should you choose to accept it, is to see fear as the teacher that it is and find the answer within the love that you are.

Blessings as you express yourself fearlessly in the world and awaken to *everything you didn't know you wanted.*

In relentless devotion,
Az & Bee

P.S. We want to apologize to you, dear reader. In our intro, we promised you fucks and farts, and we failed to deliver on the farts.

So let us make it up to you now.

Benjamin's farts are masterpieces. He never hides them—always expresses them fully and unapologetically. Azrya admits that, yes, sometimes they have triggered her, especially when she's spooning him from behind naked in bed and can literally feel the hot air on her leg. But those flatulent triggers are teachers, too. They have taught her a deeper level of devotion than she ever knew possible.

After all, to truly love someone is to embrace the full spectrum of who they are; fears, fucks, farts, and all. Right?

(At least that's the story Azrya's telling herself).

Now, we are complete. Blessings on your journey.

THE 5 STEPS TO INTEGRATING YOUR SHADOW AND BEQOMING FULLY ALIVE

Like all internal processes, especially those that involve an emotional charge, these 5 steps aren't always going to work in a linear fashion. Use them more as a guideline, not a hard rule. This is about creating space for your process and giving yourself permission to be fully present with yourself.

Full-spectrum aliveness comes as a byproduct of the practice of presence, which simply means being fully engaged in What Is *right now*.

These 5 steps aim to simplify this practice of presence and create a reliable structure you can apply to every challenging emotional situation. The more you practice, the more you increase your EQ (emotional intelligence), the more your ability to truly savor the richness of your full-spectrum aliveness increases.

Here the 5 steps at a glance:

1. See it
2. Feel it
3. Express it
4. Name it
5. Make love to it

THE CONTAINER

Before you begin this practice, we recommend that you create "the container" by designating a private space where you can freely express yourself without being disturbed. The potency of this space can be amplified by lighting a candle and adding meaningful objects that are sacred to you. A yoga mat and/or meditation cushion are helpful to include as well. Once you are comfortable in your container, turn your phone on silent and set a timer for 15 minutes, then commit to following the 5 steps without any distractions.

You can use the written instructions below, or download the guided audio track at *www.BEQOMING.me/tools.*

STEP 1: SEE IT

Everything begins with awareness. Close your eyes and take a few deep breaths, giving yourself permission to arrive fully in the present moment. As you deepen your inhales and exhales, bring your attention deeper and deeper into your body and begin to illuminate what is most alive inside of you. This could be racing thoughts, a specific sensation, or a feeling.

STEP 2: FEEL IT

The emotional charge associated with what is present will likely be intensifying now. This is good! Keep breathing into it. Like pointing a magnifying glass at it, allow it to expand and use your breath to dissolve the urge to resist and distract yourself from it, no matter how uncomfortable it might be to feel it. The feeling contains invaluable information, as long as you are willing to meet it. Whether it's anxiety, shame, exhaustion, or numbness, let it be felt *fully*.

STEP 3: EXPRESS IT

Once you have established a connection with the most prominent feeling(s), it's time to let them express themselves through you. This could be a verbal expression, such as "I'm so disappointed" or "I feel utterly lost and alone." It could also be a guttural sound, a whimper, a cry, a laugh, or a scream. It could be shaking or trembling. Whatever the expression, allow it to be heard fully for as long as needed.

STEP 4: NAME IT

Who is this part of you that needs to be felt? As you witness its expression, recognize that this is likely a part of you that is starved for love. Tune into where this part of you originated, then give it a name. If you associate it with a childhood version of yourself, perhaps there's a nickname you used to be called that fits. It can also be something like "the unseen little girl," "the wounded little boy," or if it feels more like a grown-up aspect of you, it could be "the distracted father" or "the imposter." Naming this part of yourself is a powerful act of de-identifying with it. Yes, this is a part of you. But it isn't *all* of you. It's simply an aspect of you that you've shamed and rejected that is ready to be integrated. Naming it also helps you identify and embrace it much more easily the next time it pops up, until eventually it just becomes another character within the pantheon of avatars that make up the wholeness of who you are.

(For the advanced version of this step, find the Avatar Exercise at *www.B≡QOMING.me/tools*.)

STEP 5: MAKE LOVE TO IT

Once you've named it, explore opening your heart to this part of you now. Dissolve any shame or self-judgment by recognizing that this part of you has attempted to use whatever emotions you identified in Step 1 as a defense mechanism to avoid being hurt further. Reclaim your power by taking full responsibility for its innocent attempt to protect you. Embrace this part of yourself now by asking what it needs from you, and then giving it. Often simply being seen and heard is enough. Let this part know it is safe, welcome, and worthy of your love. As you "make love to it" by finding pleasure in receiving the healing power of your own presence, observe the energy transform into something new. Breathe that in, nice and deep. Allow it to marinate inside of you. The more time you can take with this, the better.

INTEGRATE

When you are done, open your eyes and write down your observations. How do you feel now? Even if there was just a one-degree shift in your vibration, that's a huge accomplishment.

To continually, actively, and consciously choose to repeat these 5 steps is to begin to surf the leading edge of your consciousness, rather than being pummeled by the force of its wave, crashing head first into the rocks or getting stuck on a sand dune. At first, you'll be wobbly and take a few spills. The more deeply you are willing to feel, the more quickly you'll get the hang of it and start to stabilize. Eventually you'll feel firm on your feet and be able to actually enjoy the exhilarating sensation of the wind in your hair and the sun on your skin as you ride through the ebbs and flows of your light and your shadow. Then you'll start to go looking for a bigger wave to surf, one that challenges you and forces you out of your comfort zone yet again!

Life will relentlessly invite you to expand, evolve, and grow. The more willing you are to participate in the curriculum it has prepared for you, the more alive you will feel.

ACKNOWLEDGMENTS

JOINT ACKNOWLEDGMENTS

Deep love to our Soul Family. We wouldn't be who we are today without you: Blu, Briana, Zahara, Issa, Adrian, Anail, Bear Heart, Aubrey, Vylana, Peter, Maria, Ruben, Leigh & Archie.

Sweet Mars, thank you for bringing so much juicy love into our lives.

Jenny for bringing the cover design to life. Raven for midwifing this book through the final edit and Scribe for guiding us through the process , with special thanks to Natalie.

Special thanks to Feyzi, Christina, Erik & Jeff for being the first to trust us in the B Ξ Q O MI N G process.

A huge blast of humble gratitude to the Indigenous people who preserved the sacred plant medicine traditions for thousands of years in the face of great adversity and are sharing them with us today.

Thank you to The Second Mountain, our home, our sacred land, and all the ancestors who came before us. May you continue to thrive, flourish, and share your medicine with those who walk upon you.

AZRYA'S ACKNOWLEDGMENTS

From the bottom of my heart I want to say Thank You to...

Benjamin for being my everything. For seeing me so clearly and choosing me so fully. For giving yourself so completely to this union. For remembering your creative genius and for your incredibly high standards. In some ways, this entire book is a love letter to you.

Mom for birthing me at home, feeding me organic, plant-based food well before it was trendy, exposing me to spirituality and expanded ways of thinking, and always empowering me to trust my own inner guidance and break the rules.

Dad for sharing your passion for film and music, for the endlessly interesting conversations and for the goodness of your heart.

Adam for being my original catalyst for transformation, introducing me to the wonderful world of psychedelics and plant medicines, and the decade of collaborative magic and expansion we shared in our partnership.

Gysel for embracing me as your sister-mama and finding me—once again—in this lifetime to share another dance.

Grisel for opening your heart to me from the very beginning and teaching me what devotion means.

Steel for being the coolest kid I know and continuing to let me into your magical inner world.

Bella for welcoming me into the family, despite our differences. I feel your love and it is medicine to me.

My MissAyas (Blu, Zahara & Briana) for being my ride-or-die soul sisters in all of the many dimensions we traverse. Thank you for being my mirrors, my anchors, and my muses.

Adrian, Anáil & Rachel for showing up right when I needed you most and believing and investing in me and our shared Soul mission in all of the ways.

Nina and Sandra for loving and celebrating me across continents for all of these years. Ich bin so dankbar dass es euch gibt.

Liana for sharing the magic sauce that is you.

Andrea, Amber, Heike & Jonathan and Justin for illuminating my blind spots and helping me to quantum leap through your guidance and reflections.

@AmirImage for capturing our love in the photo on the back cover.

Serendipity for showing me how to Queen and gifting me with the privilege of admiring and adoring your magnificence.

My many plant, animal, and human teachers for reminding me of who I truly am.

And all of the other incredible souls that have touched me and made this journey of B ≡ Q O M I N G possible.

Thank you life. For your intelligence. Your grace. And your full spectrum perfection.

BEE'S ACKNOWLEDGMENTS

Everything I am and everything I believe was forged through the relationships of my life. I would like to thank the following people and organizations:

Azrya, who could have written this book, in some form, without me. But instead relentlessly insisted that I embrace a creative side of myself I did not know was there. It has been such a great honor and privilege to co-create this with you. Thank you for allowing me to love you so completely. Thank you for loving me so uncon-ditionally. I adore you.

Bella & Bello, my parents, for teaching me what it means to be unwavering in the frequency of love and always having my back.

Grisel for being such a dear friend and loving and devoted mother to our two children and for gifting us with the word "Unfuckwithable."

Gysel, the light of my life, for always being real, vulnerable, and authentic with me.

Steel for his beautiful spirit and being such a profound teacher to me.

Andy, Karla, Solara & Quinn for all the beautiful memories.

Yolanda and Carlos for taking such good care of my family.

My Alder Junto brothers (Michael D., Reza J., Brian F., Michael M., Roman T., Paul M. & Jason J.) and the rest of the epic management team at Alder.

My YPO LA Chapter, especially the various forum members I had over the years (special thanks to Jon H. for leading the way and inspiring me, through the lifeline he built, to create the B Ξ Q O M I N G Operating System).

My Vistage forum and Beth A., our fearless leader and coach. She held space for me through some incredibly challenging, exciting, and transformative years.

Jason, Jeff, Josh, David, Julio, Abraham, thank you for so many years of friendship and adventure.

Art F. for his friendship and all the juicy real estate deals over the years.

Olga for loving me so deeply and for all the curriculum that our relationship was.

Jenny for holding space for me during the depth of my darkness.

Brianna, Bear Heart, Blu, Z & Tao for being and bringing so much powerful medicine into my life.

Adrian & Archie for all your support and love on our adventure in Peru.

All the beautiful women who shared their sexual energy with me, thank you for the amazing memories. (I am truly sorry for all the times I misled, coerced, and manipulated.) May you be blessed, held, and loved as you truly deserve.

Doug M., Alfred O. & the thousands of team members that served with us at Fiesta Foods.